Lessons of the Wild

For: Frank Marek
Best Wishes!
Ed Andersen
6·12·09

Lessons of the Wild

Learning from the Wisdom of Nature

EDWIN L. ANDERSEN

WIPF & STOCK · Eugene, Oregon

LESSONS OF THE WILD
Learning from the Wisdom of Nature

Copyright © 2009 Edwin L. Andersen. All rights reserved. Except for brief quotations in critical publications or reviews, no part of this book may be reproduced in any manner without prior written permission from the publisher. Write: Permissions, Wipf and Stock Publishers, 199 W. 8th Ave., Suite 3, Eugene, OR 97401.

Wipf & Stock
A Division of Wipf and Stock Publishers
199 W. 8th Ave., Suite 3
Eugene, OR 97401
www.wipfandstock.com

ISBN 13: 978-1-60608-346-8

Manufactured in the U.S.A.

Biblical citations are taken from the King James Version of the Holy Bible

"Ask Me," copyright 1977, 1998 the Estate of William Stafford, reprinted from The Way It Is: New & Selected Poems with the permission of Graywolf Press, Saint Paul, Minnesota.

To Debbie,
For showing me the beauty
of the inner wilderness

Vernal Falls in Yosemite National Park, Circa 1880
Although reproduced by I. W. Taber, this photograph was probably the work of famed pioneering photographer Carlton E. Watkins

Contents

Preface ix

1 Wilderness Lost 1

2 The Duckbuilder's Way 30

3 A Redoubtable Journey 52

4 Teacher Rattlesnake 65

5 Passages 84

6 Crossing the Abyss 100

7 The Seventh Lesson 118

Twenty-third Psalm: A Wilderness Interpretation 131
The Wilderness Prayer 132
Bibliography 133

Preface

THE SUN WAS GENTLY sinking in the gold and crimson sky, and my eyes were drawn to the soft silhouette of the western hills beyond the shimmering waters. Reeds bent compliantly before the persistent December winds, and the fragrances of the marsh swirled all about me. The scene was punctuated by the sights and sounds of scattered flocks of migrating ducks and geese. Only Nature can paint such a sublime scene in just the blink of an eye. I was an anxious observer—an intruder—on the canvas of one of Nature's fleeting masterpieces.

As a flock of green-winged teal, among the most beautiful of birds on the wing, came headlong towards me, I sensed something out of the ordinary—something that I had never felt before. I lowered my 12-gauge shotgun, ejected its shells, and placed it by my side. From the blind next to mine my father asked, "Not going to shoot anymore today?" Trying to conceal the tears in my eyes, I replied, "Never again!" Although moments like this had happened to me before, this was the first time that I was conscious of being taught one of Nature's essential lessons.

Certain events in a man's life can be especially instructive, as if they were markers along the trail. We don't always immediately recognize these signs, and if we do, it is usually later on in our journey when we are older and wise enough to ponder the meaning of the years. While in Nature's world, we might appreciate her movements and her beauty, but we can't possibly predict how a wilderness encounter might alter the course of the rest of our lives. The hunting experience that I have told about took place more than thirty years ago, and I have not fired a gun since; not for any activist reasons, but because I learned something once in a duck blind that opened my eyes to life on a grander scale. Experiences like mine are not uncommon. Many of us have had them.

Parker Palmer, popular Quaker writer and thinker, speaks eloquently of the timeless wisdom underlying Thomas Merton's conception of the *hidden wholeness of all things*.

> In the visible world of Nature, a great truth is concealed in plain sight; diminishment and beauty, darkness and light, death and life are not opposites. They are held together in the paradox of hidden wholeness.[1]

As a young man, Merton became disenchanted with the shallowness of secular society, and being richly influenced by ascetic ideals, he sought his vocation as a monk. During the 1940s and 50s, while living in solitude at the Abbey of Gethsemani, nestled among the trees and hills and streams of rural Kentucky, Merton penned numerous books. These books contain deeply moving accounts of his encounters not only in Nature, but in the wilderness of his soul. Perhaps no writer in recent memory captured the raw essences and the connectedness of wild places more compellingly than did Thomas Merton.

Merton's "hidden wholeness" is grounded in a profound consciousness of the sublime relationship of all things to one another. Thus, if we seek to become more like whom we were created to be—our authentic selves—then we will have begun to do something vitally important. *Lessons of the Wild: Learning from the Wisdom of Nature* supposes that we are part of an invisible web of life, and that Nature's lessons can help to move us toward becoming better men. Better men make for a better world, and a better world is something worth striving for. Hopefully, this book offers some fresh ways of looking at Nature and challenges the reader to look deeply into his, or her, own inner wilderness.

There are numerous stories in this book, some of which may appear to be more than extraordinary. Perhaps they seem so because most of the characters told about are such ordinary folks. How these people came so fortuitously into my life and why they so willingly shared their journeys, I will never quite comprehend. But I am assured that each of their experiences actually took place and that they have been related in as factual a detail as memory and the passage of time permit. None of the portrayals are fictional, and none of their names have been changed.

Lessons of the Wild is also a book about managing transitions. During my last six years in the corporate world, I counseled men and women who were moving from one stage of their work lives to another. While these life shifts were career related, they had notable reverberations into other aspects of these people's lives. In many cases, the people I met experienced

---

1. Palmer, *Let Your Life Speak*, 99.

emotional and psychological distress, followed by periods of remarkable healing. I remain convinced that the lessons we learn in the wild can help prepare us to successfully manage difficult transitions—especially in the complex passages from childhood to adulthood, and from middle age to an "age of wisdom."

I am thankful for a number of influential thinkers, who by their writings have helped to shape my view of life and nurtured in me a richer understanding of my place in the vast expanse of the universe. First and foremost among these thinkers are Thomas Merton and John Muir. Time and again I have been richly rewarded by reading Merton's writings, especially his *Seeds of Contemplation*. Muir's colorful accounts of his life in the woods are unsurpassed; works, like *My First Summer in the Sierra* and *The Mountains of California*, published more than a century ago, are as fresh as a field of diasies. I am indebted to writers like Loren Eiseley, Annie Dillard, Wendell Berry, Rachel Carson, and the many others who have given me their unique insights into the wholeness hidden in all things. Among others, I have borrowed liberally from the wisdom of T. S. Eliot, Parker Palmer, Huston Smith, Robert Bly, Gerald May, John Eldredge, and Richard Rohr—every one a trailblazer in our amazing journey through the wilderness.

My family and friends have heartily endorsed the writing of this book. My wife, Debbie, and our daughters, Michelle and Jennifer, have unwittingly given me the courage to write. Michelle is a college English teacher, who has made me feel worthy as an author and has lovingly kept me focused on the finish line. Some of my fondest memories will always be of days on the softball field and on the trail, hiking and backpacking with Jennifer, who now also has followed her mother into the teaching profession. Books do not get written without great sacrifices being made by those around us. I am particularly grateful to Debbie for sharing so many wonderful years with me and giving me two beautiful children, but also for selflessly granting me so much time in solitude. There is something special about belonging to a family of teachers.

This book would not have been written were it not for the faith and enthusiasm of dear friends like Russ Giambelluca, Steve Sample, Michael Smythe, John Wipf, Chris Cisneros, Julia Freeman, and the rest. Although Steve cautioned me some years ago that writing a book was the most difficult thing he had ever attempted, his words became beacons of encouragement. He has been a gracious mentor to me along the way. Thanks also to Anita Sorensen, a stranger who helped me to remember that the wilderness is a place for all of us, and that perhaps there is something in these pages that will resonate with women, as well as with men.

Whenever I open this book, I will hold precious memories of my friend Eric Remelmeyer, who faced death with remarkable courage and vision. In his last few days, as he prepared to take the heavenward trail, Eric listened thoughtfully as I read excerpts from the manuscript to him. In those fading moments, he taught me that no man suffers alone and that death is a natural obstacle if we are to cross over into the ultimate wilderness. When I saw him for the final time, this extraordinary person suggested that when his health improved we should spend a few days together in the wild. We will, Eric! Someday, we will.

Lessons of the Wild has been on my heart for a long time. Now that it has come forth, I earnestly hope that it will speak to readers in a meaningful way, much like the way that Nature has spoken to me on so many occasions. In the final analysis, this book is an invitation—an invitation to renew our ties with the first place of our belonging. *Lessons of the Wild* is your personal call to revisit the wilderness, and to remember what it is like to touch the stars.

Ed Andersen
Arcadia, California

1

Wilderness Lost

There is no one on the planet who does not lose when wilderness is lost.

—Bob Brown

BY ITS VERY ESSENCE, the word *wilderness* defies adequate definition. Aldo Leopold, legendary conservationist and philosopher, once described Nature's wilderness as a "continuous stretch of country preserved in its natural state, open to lawful hunting and fishing, big enough to absorb a two weeks pack trip."[1] Parts of Alaska, Australia's outback, and the Antarctic are places that still fit Leopold's description, but wilderness areas of this sort are seldom seen by the average person. As the physical world has been altered by the hand of man, so too has our understanding of wilderness. Today we might best describe wilderness as a place where there is little or no evidence of human intrusion.

Wilderness is often experienced in remote places, but it may also be discovered just beyond our doors in a bed of flowers or under an elm tree. It is accessible in the vacant lot at the end of the street and in a Napa Valley vineyard. Verifiable accounts from the wilderness have been made by Himalayan conquerors, as well as by day-dwellers on city park benches. Barefoot impressions in the wet sand of a crowded beach can reveal the presence of a wilderness traveler, as prominently as any boot

1. Nash, *Wilderness and the American Mind*, 186.

print on a secluded mountain trail. And as assuredly as there is a physical wilderness, there is also a wilderness within each one of us. It is this inner wilderness, so intimately connected with the wilderness outside, which is most elusive.

We humans are children of the wilderness. Countless generations of our early ancestors were born in wild places and were long held firmly in Nature's embrace. At the dawn of history, as Roderick Nash observes, "There was no meaningful distinction between man and Nature, no dualism."[2] Primitives were wanderers, hunters, and gatherers, following flocks and herds of wild game, seeking to furnish their basic needs wherever the vagaries of Nature might carry them. Though at a great physical disadvantage, *Homo sapiens* possessed one truly extraordinary gift that was to elevate him above the rest of his animal kin—the human brain.

In time, with ingenuity and through innovation, man forged tools that helped make good his escape from Mother Nature. With advancements such as the wheel, the axe, and the plow, nomadic peoples no longer foraged widely over great distances but established permanent settlements in the savannas, steppes, and river valleys of the world. Humans became more "civilized," but as they did, their essential relationship with Mother Nature began to shift from familial to adversarial. Forests would no longer be seen as places to live, but rather as sources of lumber and barriers to agriculture. The same is true for rivers and streams, which were dammed and diverted for irrigation and commerce. Wild animals were domesticated and their physical power was harnessed to do the heavy work that man was ill-suited for. By the time the Pilgrims landed in the New World on their "errand into the wilderness,"[3] the total conquest of Nature had become an obsession, and America was a land of seemingly limitless opportunity. There were forests to clear, roads to build, and destinies to be made manifest.

When Henry David Thoreau published a memoir of his time at Walden Pond in the mid-1800s, man's break with Nature was nearly complete; the wilderness had become a terrifying unknown for most Americans. Thoreau was a close personal friend of Ralph Waldo Emerson and was well

---

2. Ibid., xiii.

3. Rev. Samuel Danforth used this expression in a 1670 address to delegates of the Massachusetts General Court. See Danforth, "A Brief Recognition of New-England's Errand into the Wilderness," 2. For a detailed examination, see Miller, *Errand into the Wilderness*.

established in New England's social circles, so when he reported back from the wilderness there was more than just casual interest.

Although the pond was but a mere mile or two from the busy town of Concord, it seemed to the civilized world that Thoreau had visited some distant unspoiled territory. Nothing could have been further from the truth. Though he records, "I have a great deal of company in my house; especially in the morning, when nobody calls,"[4] Thoreau surely didn't find much pure solitude at Walden Pond, which was a popular four-season recreation site for the Concord community. Picnickers, fishermen, ice skaters, and numerous local characters, many of whom are mentioned in *Walden*, regularly made their way there. The area was much less wooded in Thoreau's time than at present, as the forest trees had been thinned by woodcutters and home builders. Even without all the earmarks of a true wilderness site, Walden Pond provided a useful backdrop for Thoreau's symbolic return to Nature.

Henry David Thoreau was drawn into the Massachusetts woods by the same mysterious force Nature has exerted on men since the earliest times. Secluded within Nature, and within each one of us, are sacred wilderness places. These inward and outward places are hopelessly intertwined and operate like magnets to pull us back into harmony with Nature. Together, these wildernesses have combined to play an important role in the dramas of history. It was into these solitudes that the founders of our major religious faiths retreated to find their callings. More than three millennia ago, a man named Moses, who had been inspired by a mountaintop experience, successfully led the Hebrews out of bondage in Egypt. In their quest to discover the "land of milk and honey,"[5] these people wandered through the Mediterranean wilderness for more than forty years. The Jews have emerged from this marathon journey as one of the world's most enduring people, contributing much to the fabric of our art and culture.

We are told that Confucius (551–479 B.C.), the First Teacher of the Chinese people, was an archer, a hunter, and a fisherman.[6] Whereas no reports of his sporting exploits survive, we can safely assume that much of his wisdom was acquired through his experiences in Nature. Confucius's contemporary, Siddhārtha Gautama (Buddha), abruptly abandoned his

---

4. Thoreau, *Walden*, 148.

5. Ex 3:8.

6. The archer, hunter, and fisherman are prominent figures in stories attributed to Confucius.

life as an Indian nobleman for an ascetic existence in the forest, where after six years he found enlightenment while sitting under a wild fig tree. Today, with more than 350 million adherents, Buddhism has become one of our most influential religious traditions. Another extraordinary leader was the Prophet Mohammed (A.D. 570–632), who spent countless hours praying in a cave near the city of Mecca, in what is now Saudi Arabia. It was in this wild setting that he discovered his destiny, and over fourteen centuries later Islam is the fastest growing of the world's major religions.

The Holy Bible records that Jesus Christ fasted for forty days in the austerity of the Judean wilderness in preparation for a remarkable three years of public ministry. Today, about one-third of the planet's inhabitants claim to be Christians. Ironically, the coming of the "King of Kings" was heralded not by some great Delphic oracle, but by a wild man who lived in the desert, clothed in camel hair and living on a diet of locusts and honey.

Throughout recorded time, Nature has been the setting for initiation rites that prepare young men to assume the mantle of manhood. Primitive initiations generally took the form of banishment of the initiate into the wilderness and often involved physical pain, such as piercing and circumcision. Although these rites have taken more humane forms in modern times, they are still being practiced. For example, there are numerous organizations that offer retreats and training based on the ancient Native American practice of *Vision Quest*, where the subject must subsist alone in the wild until he knows his sacred name and comes face-to-face with the Great Spirit. Many men and women have returned from these quests with a deeper knowledge of self and with a better sense of direction for their lives.

Robert Bly's *Iron John* and *Adam's Return* by Richard Rohr are must reads for a better understanding of the practice and importance of traditional male initiation. Bly tells the story of Iron John, which originated with the Grimm Brothers in the early 1800s. It is a cryptic tale of a boy and a hairy man who has been captured by one of the king's knights at the bottom of a lake in the heart of the forest. The boy is coaxed into releasing Iron John, who becomes his unlikely mentor as he passes through the stages of initiation, attains manhood, and wins the hand of the king's beautiful daughter. As the story reaches its climax, a nobleman of great stature arrives at the wedding feast and addresses the groom, saying: "I am Iron John, who through an enchantment became turned into a Wild Man.

You have freed me from that enchantment. All the treasure that I own will from now on belong to you."[7]

The story of Iron John raises several important questions. Who is this Wild Man, and why is he found in the depths of the forest? Why is he so difficult to find? How is it that it took a boy to lift the spell that was cast on Iron John? Answers to these questions may become clear as we journey together through the pages of this book.

Richard Rohr is the founding director for the Center for Action Contemplation in Albuquerque, New Mexico. He believes that male initiation rites teach five important lessons, or "promises," as he calls them:

- Life is hard
- You are not that important
- Your life is not about you
- You are not in control
- You are going to die

Despite what Rohr admits is "the seemingly negative character of these five truths," they illustrate just how far we have drifted from the conventional wisdom of our forbearers, and how much work lies ahead in reestablishing virtue as a guiding force in human endeavors. Rohr offers this observation: "One wonders if history would have taken the violent and oppressive forms it has if generations of men had continued to learn these five truths experientially."[8] As we will see, there is a striking synchronicity between the five promises of male initiation and the lessons that Nature teaches us in the wild.

THE DISAPPEARING WILDERNESS

However one conceives of wilderness, there is irrefutable evidence that the natural landscape has been diminishing at a gathering pace. *Acid rain*, *greenhouse gas*, and *global warming* are terms that have only recently come into our vernacular and they herald serious implications for the future of planet Earth.

In less than one hundred years, most of our forested lands have disappeared. Here in the United States, by some estimates, we have now lost

7. Bly, *Iron John*, 259.
8. Rohr, *Adam's Return*, 32–33.

as much as ninety-five percent of our old growth forests.[9] Worldwide the figure is less, but it is reported that with the prodigious rate of deforestation in the developing nations, our terrestrial home could be thoroughly depleted of old growth trees by the end of this century. In many countries, including the United States and Canada, forward thinking growers and lumber producers have partnered with government and conservationists in establishing our forests as a truly renewable resource. But it takes a tree a long time to grow, and we will not soon replace the old growth forests of our grandfathers.

Most of the world's wild rivers have been dammed to provide hydroelectric power and reserves of suitable drinking water. Just one-third of the planet's 177 major rivers remain free-flowing, unimpeded by dams or other barriers. Only twenty-one of these actually run freely from their source to the sea, while the others are large tributaries of rivers like the Congo and Amazon.[10] Rivers and streams feed the fragile ecosystems that sustain life on the planet, and as such are key indicators of the overall health of our environment. As more and more sources of fresh drinking water become threatened, preservation and responsible water management will become increasingly important to human survival.

While the disappearing wilderness has created complications for humankind, it has had a devastating effect on the world's wildlife. With the destruction of habitat, compounded by the added burden of pollution and pesticides, many species of animal life are endangered or have disappeared altogether. I once read that John J. Audubon, leading nineteenth century ornithologist, observed a flock of passenger pigeons so immense that it blackened the sky for days. During the mid-1800s, the total population of passenger pigeons may have reached five billion individuals and comprised up to forty percent of total bird life in North America.[11] However, the combination of forest habitat destruction and unregulated hunting led to the demise of the passenger pigeon, which officially became extinct in 1914.

As recently as the 1950s, ducks and geese migrating between Canada and the United States along the Pacific and Atlantic flyways were so prolific that flocks numbering in the tens of thousands—even hundreds of

---

9. Supporting data may be obtained online at: http://www.nationalgeographic.com, http://www.greenpeace.org, and other related websites.

10. World Wildlife Federation, "Free Flowing Rivers," 3.

11. Schorger, *The Passenger Pigeon*, 201–4.

thousands—were regularly seen. But as the marshlands supporting these large flocks were drained for cultivation, the numbers of migratory birds declined precipitously. Hastening their disappearance was the emergence of a sophisticated illegal hunting industry that supplied restaurants with ducks, geese, and cranes. During the 1930s and 1940s, the demand for wildfowl was so high in cities like San Francisco and Los Angeles that black market hunters reaped enormous profits, even as the Great Depression bankrupted the country. Hugh M. Worcester, a game management officer in California and Nevada at the time, recalls:

> I have a record of two market hunters who sold $20,000 in water fowl, pheasants, quail, deer, and trout. They began the latter part of July on upland game and fish and were caught in the middle of the fall duck-hunting season. Another prominent market hunter—just before leaving for the Federal penitentiary—got in a confessional mood and informed the U.S. District Attorney that, during the several years before he was caught, he had killed over 50,000 ducks himself.[12]

On Thanksgiving Day in 1961, my family and I caught a glimpse of what it must have been like to live in that bygone age when Nature's plenitude and vitality were in full bloom. My father was at the wheel of our Ford station wagon as we hurriedly made our way through the San Joaquin Valley to celebrate with relatives. Suddenly, Dad rammed on the brakes and the car came screeching to an awkward halt. Blanketing the field before us, arrayed in their magnificent winter plumage, was the largest flock of Ring-neck pheasants that one could possibly imagine. Spread out over several hundred yards, the birds were feeding voraciously on the seed and grubs that had been turned up in the newly plowed field. The damp clay soil of the San Joaquin stuck to the feet of the birds like glue, and most of them could scarcely keep their balance as they gorged themselves on the Thanksgiving feast. For a moment we sat there in silent amazement, as if peering back into history through the porthole of Nature's time machine. Then Dad got out of the car and after carefully estimating their numbers, declared: "Must be 1500 pheasants!" It is doubtful that any of us will ever again see a flock of wild pheasants as large as this one, but it was not so long ago that scenes like this were commonplace.

---

12. Worcester, *Hunting the Lawless*, 59.

It was but a few generations ago that unnumbered grizzly bears, elk, antelope, and bison ranged widely across America. Nearly everyone knows of the slaughter of the buffalo (*Bison bison*) during the western migration of the pioneers across the Great Plains in the late nineteenth century. While tens of thousands were shot to feed the men who worked on the transcontinental railroad, and later from trains and wagons for sheer sport, the near extermination of the bison was accomplished largely as part of a strategy by the United States military to force the capitulation of the American Indian. In just a two year period between 1872 and 1874, it is estimated that over seven million buffalo were killed.[13] Were it not for the alarm sounded by a cadre of influential military leaders and government officials, the bison might easily have met the same fate as the passenger pigeon.

It took hunters only a few decades to eliminate the grizzly bear (*Ursus arctos horribilis*) from most of the contiguous United States. Once living in every region of the country, only a handful of these magnificent animals can now be found in Montana, Wyoming, and Idaho. By the early 1900s, the American elk (*Cervus elephus*) population was so decimated that domestication was deemed the last resort to save them from extinction. Once the widest ranging member of the American deer family, the great elk herds have been relegated to the Rocky Mountain region, with a few others scattered throughout the rest of the United States.

Population estimates of Pronghorn Antelope (*Antilocapra americana*), which blanketed the American frontier in the 1870s, simply boggle the imagination. With numbers gauged at between fifty and seventy million, this fleet-footed mammal was probably the most populous big game animal then living on the continent. One passenger on the transcontinental railroad credibly reported a herd of antelope that stretched continuously for more than seventy miles. According to the North American Pronghorn Association in Rawlins, Wyoming, antelope carcasses could be purchased in some western towns for pennies. When the market became so glutted that hunters could not even give their kills away, thousands of pronghorns that had been ruthlessly gunned down were simply left to rot. Though once reduced to less than ten thousand animals, the current antelope population seems to be holding steady at about one million.[14]

---

13. Ellis, *General Pope and U.S. Indian Policy*, 179.
14. Hutchins, "Prairie Racer," para. 19.

As many of us can testify, the sights and sounds of wild animals are an indispensable part of the wilderness experience. In 1998, a fellow backpacker and I found ourselves without drinking water in a remote part of Yosemite National Park. Celebrating our fiftieth birthdays, and looking to prove that we were still worthy of Nature's rigors, we had planned an ambitious five-day trek through the backcountry. On the second day out, we covered thirteen miles of mostly uphill trails. Although we religiously carry plenty of water, the hike proved to be particularly taxing, and we had exhausted our reserves. Relying on our map, we anxiously arrived at a small meadow that should have had a stream running through it. But our anxiety turned to desperation when we discovered that the stream was nothing but a mud hole. As we continued ahead we noticed that something had trampled a wide swath through the tall grass leading to a small brushy knoll about a hundred yards away. Curious though we were, our circumstances did not allow us the luxury of time to investigate, so we trudged on. Fortuitously, at the far end of the meadow we came upon a tiny trickle of water. As we began to fill our water bottles, we were startled by a thunderous noise coming from the direction of the knoll. Though neither of us had ever heard the sound of a snoring bear, it was unmistakable. We quickly finished re-supplying ourselves with water and quietly headed up the trail. It is a rare wilderness traveler who has heard a bruin snoozing contentedly in its natural habitat, and I will always cherish the memory of that unforgettable moment.

PEOPLE OF THE WILD

Primitive societies had no word for wilderness; there was no distinction between what moderns call wilderness and what primitive societies knew as their home. For the indigenous American, the world was created by the Great Spirit and the Earth has always been his mother. The Indian is a humble and grateful steward of the land, the rivers, and the forests—part of one great being with the whole of creation. But, with the settling of the West, the American Indian was inevitably forced to surrender his lands and relocate to reservations, where he stood helplessly by as settlement and industrialization changed the landscape forever.

Carol Ann Brant is a direct descendant of Chief Tyendinaga (Joseph Brant), the renowned Iroquois leader of the American Revolutionary period. She sums up the Indian's view of westernization:

> Wherever the Indian walks on the continent, the spirit of their ancestors rises from their bones in the dust of the earth and speaks in a thousand languages. The Indian knows that this is home. To the colonizers, the earth is not their Mother, it is merely a commodity to exploit, to consume, to use up, to buy and to sell for profit. The final manifestation of this attitude will be the final destruction of all—the fish and animals, the birds and insects, the trees and grasses—and *dreams*.[15]

Perhaps as well as any people on Earth, the Native American understands the meaning of a place called "home."

Hin-ma-too-ya-lat-ket, meaning "thunder traveling to lofty mountain heights," was one of the very last—and one of the most outspoken—of the great Indian chiefs. Chief Joseph, as he is better known, gained notoriety for his skilled leadership during a much publicized campaign against Federal troops during the so-called "Indian Wars" of the late 1800s. After an unprecedented flight of more than a thousand miles through Oregon, Washington, Idaho, and Montana, Joseph's beleaguered band of Nez Percé finally surrendered to General Oliver O. Howard on October 5, 1877. Joseph, who later spoke before the United States Congress, became a keynote voice of the national conscience and of the tragedy of the American Indian's vanishing way of life. He vainly hoped that the leadership in Washington would ultimately recognize the inherent rights of the Red Man and restore him to his homeland. Taken from one of his famous orations are the following words that characterize the futility of the Indian's final struggle:

> Perhaps you think the Creator sent you here to dispose of us as you see fit. If I thought you were sent by the Creator, I might be induced to think you had a right to dispose of me. Do not misunderstand me, but understand fully with reference to my affection for the land. I never said the land was mine to do with as I choose. The one who has a right to dispose of it is the one who has created it. I claim a right to live on my land and accord you the privilege to return to yours ... In the winds which pass through these aged pines we hear the moaning of their departed ghosts. And if the voices of our people could have been heard, that act would never have been done. But alas, though they stood around, they could neither be seen nor heard. Their tears fell like drops of rain. I hear my voice in the depths of the forest, but no answering voice comes back to me. All is silent around me. My

---

15. Martin, ed. *Wilderness*, 41.

words must therefore be few. I can say no more. He is silent, for he has nothing to answer when the sun goes down.[16]

Chief Joseph lived out the remainder of his years on reservations in Oklahoma and Kansas. When he died in 1904, the physician in attendance reported that the cause of death was a "broken heart."

However one views the treatment of the native people during the settling of the West, the indubitable fact remains that the frontier was mightily transformed in just the blink of an eye. No longer could one see vast herds of bison or skies blackened by millions of migrating birds. Forests gave way to farmlands, and the echo of beating drums was replaced by the sounds of the axe and the hammer. A way of life had faded away, and the voice of one of Nature's closest allies fell eerily silent.

With the dispossession of the Indian, the government of the United States found itself with little will and few resources to enforce laws protecting property rights and regulating land development. Ranchers and farmers swept in to stake their claims on former Indian territories. "Squatters" came with them, clearing trees, planting crops, and raising sheep and cattle on lands for which they had no rightful claim. Mining operations disfigured the landscape, diverting lengthy sections of rivers and streams in the pursuit of precious metals. Lumbermen acquired the timber rights to pristine forests, and with little concern for the long term consequences, denuded vast tracts of land. Trappers and hunters were constrained only by the number of pelts and game that they could transport to settlements and trading posts. This plundering of the western frontier continued almost unabated until voices of dissent slowly began to be heard. As we shall see later, we owe much to the men and women behind these voices.

LIVING WITH THE PAST

Fall Creek State Park, in the tiny mountain community of Felton, California, is home to some of the finest redwood trees on the Pacific coast. A visit here is a journey into a primeval wilderness. Beneath the towering canopy, lush ferns and colorful tropical flowers drape the fringes of timeless forest paths. The trained eye may catch a glimpse of a wary rainbow trout, camouflaged dimly against the stony bottom of a babbling brook. In wintertime, in a ritual repeated from time immemorial, a lonely steelhead braves the swollen waters in search of a mate and a place to

16. Josephy, *The Patriot Chiefs*, 7.

spawn. Like spirits from another time, bobcats, mountain lions, and black bears still haunt Fall Creek's quieter recesses. Such are visions of beauty and wonder, but along the meandering trails visitors are greeted by other more sobering sights.

Here in this magnificent place you will find hundreds of gigantic moss covered tree stumps, standing as sad memorials to a once noble race of trees felled by loggers in the late nineteenth century. Some of these evergreen trees (*Sequoia sempervirens*) must have stood more than three hundred feet tall and been more than twelve feet in diameter. The timber cutter's eye was keen indeed, for nearly all of the old growth trees are gone. If one travels far enough up the trail, the skeletal remains of the old lumber mill can still be seen, rotting away like the fallen timber that surrounds it. The Fall Creek ecosystem illuminates the staggering dichotomy between the wild forces of Nature on the one hand, and the commercial interests of civilization on the other.

Perhaps no American icon so forcefully portrays this dichotomy as does Hetch Hetchy. Tucked away in the northwest portion of Yosemite National Park, the Hetch Hetchy Valley had few visitors prior to the advent of white hunters and explorers in the 1850s. For untold generations, transient Native Americans had harvested acorns and hunted wild game in the lushness of the valley floor. For the few who saw it, the Hetch Hetchy was a wilderness place of unsurpassed magnificence.

Beginning in 1908, however, Hetch Hetchy became the focal point of a bitter dispute between the City of San Francisco and the fledgling conservationist movement in America. With the great earthquake and fire of 1906 still fresh in its memory, the city was aggressively seeking a sustainable source of water for its growing population.[17] In May, Mayor James Phelan petitioned then Secretary of the Interior, James R. Garfield, for use of the Tuolumne River watershed by the city of San Francisco. The city proposed to construct dams at Hetch Hetchy and nearby Lake Eleanor and to convert the area into a premier resort destination. The proposal was met by vehement opposition from preservationists across the country, led by prominent members of the Sierra Club and most notably by Robert Underwood Johnson, editor for the *Century Magazine*. After a

---

[17]. The Tuolumne River, which ran through the heart of the Hetch Hetchy Valley, was federally protected as part of the National Park system. It offered some of the purest drinking water in the west, and for this reason it was much coveted by San Francisco's city fathers.

protracted debate, the developers emerged victorious, and construction of the dam at Hetch Hetchy was approved by Congress. O'Shaughnessey Dam was completed in 1923 and it has been serving the needs of San Francisco ever since.

The century old controversy has been rekindled in recent years, and a movement to demolish the dam and restore the Hetch Hetchy to its wilderness state seems to be gaining considerable momentum. Although the landscape was dramatically altered by flooding the valley floor, the area was never developed as a resort. Thus, there remain many beautiful spots where one can enjoy Nature, especially along the rugged backcountry trails that traverse the granite highlands above the reservoir.

SAVING WILD PLACES

Rustic areas like Fall Creek State Park and Hetch Hetchy serve a relatively small number of people, yet the cumulative benefit of such wild places is enormous. A high percentage of Americans visit our State and National Parks each year to sightsee, camp, hike, fish, and boat. We refer to this activity as "recreation," and it is beneficial to the well-being of both individuals and of society as a whole. Recreation is *re*-creation; it is a renewal of our spirits—a reconnection to the source of our being. An afternoon spent hiking in the woods or in sitting at the edge of a mountain lake can help to remind us of who we are and where we fit into the grand scheme of the universe. With this in mind, it is difficult to dispute that the preservation of wild places is not a worthy undertaking, one vital to our future.

There have been several laudable efforts to create public awareness of Nature's importance, and of the negative impact humans can have on the environment. On Earth Day in 1971, the Keep America Beautiful Foundation aired a memorable television commercial that featured actor Iron Eyes Cody (1907–99). Cody was filmed weeping as he rode on horseback throughout the west, discovering that his ancestral home had been spoiled by trash and pollution. Cody was instantly recognizable by the American public, having played roles as an Indian in more than a hundred films, and his message had a dramatic effect. While the poignant imagery conveyed by the Keep America Beautiful campaign of the 1970s and 80s helped promote conservation, there is nothing quite like it being broadcast on television today. Although recent films and documentaries, such as *An Inconvenient Truth*, have attempted to shed light on dramatic environmental changes, the scientific community remains largely divided on how severe certain problems are and what to do about them.[18]

While millions of rural acres have come under Federal protection through legislation like the Wilderness Act of 1964 and the Wild and Scenic Rivers Act of 1968, it is essential to recognize the merits of preserving *greenspace*[19] in urban settings, too. Not long ago I read that psychiatrists in a major California city reported a disturbing rise in the incidence of clinical depression. Remarkably, the source of the problem was traced to the city's decision to remove a significant number of trees from along its streets. While there are encouraging signs that more and more communities throughout our country are recognizing the value of peaceful settings and are taking steps to facilitate access to the natural world, the urban wilderness movement is fragmentary. Likewise, most research and experiments are yet too new to greatly add to our understanding of urban greenspace.

Among the factors working against the conservation ethic is an apparent lack of reverence for Nature, which is most evident in those places that are readily accessible by motorized vehicles. I often used to hike and fish along the San Gabriel River above the Los Angeles basin, but no longer. Debris and graffiti adorning the rocks have so blighted the streamside that it has, in effect, become a rural ghetto. If you take a drive along the Truckee or Kern Rivers in California, you will see an alarming assortment of trash that includes old clothing, shoes, beer cans, broken bottles, plastic containers, candy wrappers, abandoned ice chests, and furniture; almost anything that can be transported by our mobile society is dumped there. In one small U.S. Forest Service campground that I visited in 2007, I observed enough waste to fill several large dumpsters. A generous amount of garbage and the stench of visible human feces made this "campground" a public health risk. These river areas have three common denominators: each of them is nearby to a large population, each is readily accessible by automobile, and each is heavily used for recreational purposes.

The Tonto National Forest in Arizona is a favorite destination for off-road enthusiasts from the nearby Phoenix metropolitan area. Unfortunately, many of these visitors are guilty of tearing up the park

---

18. *An Inconvenient Truth* is a 2006 documentary film that describes the effects of global warming on planet Earth. It features Al Gore, former Vice-President of the United States.

19. Greenspace is a term generally assigned to a natural or naturally landscaped area within an urban environment. Greenspace attempts to replicate conditions found in Nature, and typically contains trees, shrubs, flowers, and walking paths or trails.

with their ATV's, dumping tons of trash, and shooting firearms illegally. "In some places it looks like the apocalypse," says Arizona Sierra Club chairman, Jim Valaar.[20] With decreases in funding and reduced staff, park officials are unable to stay ahead of the problem.

The situation in the Tonto National Forest adds credence to mounting suspicions of a new and potentially lethal wilderness ethos that may be emerging amidst the latest generation of Nature's visitors. On a recent summer camping trip to a remote area of the Sierra Nevada's, my two nephews and I witnessed a first-hand example of the damage that can be caused by careless off-roaders. After a two-hour drive over an extremely bumpy road that covered a mere six miles, we arrived at a gorgeous emerald lake surrounded by a lush pine forest. Shortly after our arrival, the solitude of the mountains was interrupted by the revving sound of dirt bikes. The annoyance persisted throughout the afternoon. As we walked around the lake, we discovered that a group of young off-road enthusiasts had made a racecourse out of a lovely little meadow, thoroughly destroying its natural ambience. We also found more broken glass and litter at our campsite than I have seen in more than fifty seasons of camping.

Why do some people have such a blatant disregard for the beauty of Nature? One simple answer can be found in what is called "pride of ownership." I learned this many years ago from a veteran National Parks ranger, whom I met on a wilderness backpacking trip. We struck up a lively conversation over the campfire and spent the evening swapping tales of our times in the outdoors. When I asked him about the absence of trash and graffiti in remote places, he explained that the backpacker had paid a dear price to get there and was thus inclined to care for his natural surroundings. In general, the hiker possesses a sense of ownership in the wilderness that is not universally shared by those who have motorized access to outdoor recreation areas.

SIGNS OF HOPE

Reverence for Nature is a matter of respect, requiring a concerted effort to educate our citizens about the value of preserving wilderness. Scouting and Summer Camps throughout our country are at the forefront of this effort. *The Official Boy Scout Handbook* has sold tens of millions of copies since it was first published in 1910. It is a guidebook for boys, not only

---

20. Mendoza, "National Forests Battle Trash, ATV's," para. 16.

to learn the essentials of becoming an outdoorsman, but to acquire the essentials of becoming a man. It says, "Scouting is far more than fun in the outdoors, hiking, and camping. Scouting is a way of life. Scouting is growing into responsible manhood, learning to be of service to others."[21]

"Eagle" is scouting's highest award and only one boy in twenty attains this rank. To do so, a young man must meet high standards of leadership, outdoor skills, and service to his community. As a final prerequisite, Eagle Scout candidates must devise, plan, and execute a Leadership Service Project benefiting a local organization other than the Boy Scouts. Many candidates choose a wilderness site for their project, sometimes assisting the Forest Service and the Bureau of Land Management in rebuilding trails, planting trees, and restoring campgrounds. Outcomes of the service project can have a lasting impact on a teenage boy as he matures into manhood and makes his way through life. Eagle scouts have been so recognized for their service to America that the Eagle badge may be worn on a United States military uniform. No other civilian award merits this distinction.

For more than sixty-five years, Outward Bound has operated schools to educate young people in wilderness settings. Their mission statement reads: "To inspire character development and self-discovery in people of all ages and walks of life through challenge and adventure and to impel them to achieve more than they ever thought possible, to show compassion for others and to actively engage in creating a better world."[22] With more than half a million alumni, Outward Bound serves as a beacon of hope in educating our youth in the important work of preserving wilderness.

The National Outdoor Leadership School (NOLS) was founded in 1965 by Paul Petzoldt, an innovative mountaineer, who first climbed Wyoming's Grand Teton peak wearing cowboy boots. "Paul Petzoldt's idea was simple: take people into the wilderness for an extended period of time, teach them the right things, feed them well and when they walk out of the mountains, they will be skilled leaders."[23] NOLS offers expeditions lasting up to a month, and to date it has graduated more than 75,000 young leaders. Paul Petzoldt was among the first to actively recognize that wilderness survival skills are the same skills as those needed to succeed back in the civilized world.

21. *The Official Boy Scout Handbook*, 9.
22. Outward Bound, "Mission Statement," homepage.
23. National Outdoor Leadership School, "About Us," n.p.

The National Rifle Association (NRA) is dedicated to offering safe, responsible gun control programs to the public. As it has long been the target of environmental groups and gun control activists, the conservative NRA describes itself as, "a major political force and as America's foremost defender of Second Amendment rights."[24] Whatever one's position on the politics of the NRA and gun regulation, there is little doubt that this organization has led the way in educating young people about the safe use of firearms. Each year, the NRA supports over one million youths nationwide in sport shooting events, primarily through affiliates like 4-H and the Jaycees. The Sierra Club, The American Camp Association, and the YMCA are among other notable organizations that offer extensive programs for environmental education and activism.

LOSING TOUCH

Notwithstanding the efforts of summer camps, Boy Scouts, and the rest, there are signs of a marked decline in physical contact with Nature. Evidence for this trend can be found in the annual report of the National Wildlife Federation (NWF), which publishes statistics on the numbers of hunting and fishing licenses issued each year in the United States. During the decade from 1990 to 2000, while the U.S. population grew by 13.2 percent, the number of licensed hunters and fishermen dropped by four percent. Table 1.1, below, shows just how little change there has been in the sale of sporting licenses since 1975.

Table 1.1 Hunting and fishing licenses sold annually in the United States

Licenses Sold (millions)	1975	1980	1985	1990	1995	2000
Hunting	16.5	16.3	15.9	15.8	15.2	15.0
Fishing	27.5	27.8	28.7	30.7	30.3	29.6
Total	44.0	44.1	44.6	46.5	45.5	44.6

Source: *National Wildlife Federation*.[25]

24. National Rifle Association, "A Brief History of the NRA," para. 14.

25. The NWF began in 1936, when President Franklin D. Roosevelt convened the first North American Wildlife Conference. With over five million members, the NWF has established itself as a leading voice for conservation and wildlife habitat preservation.

On a *per capita* basis, the actual number of sportsmen has decreased significantly over the past thirty years. Restricted access to fields and streams, shrinking game availability, economic considerations, and lifestyle choices are among the factors contributing to this trend away from hunting and fishing. Determined animal rights and gun control activists have also made their voices heard in recent times and are probable factors in this decline.

While camping, hiking, and biking—quintessential American outdoor pursuits—are still the top choices for recreation, much has happened to change the way we experience the great outdoors. In the past, Americans hitched up their trailers, loaded their cars, and headed for a rustic campground in the mountains. Nowadays, "fewer young people are participating in such traditional outdoor activities as hiking, opting instead for the thrills of off-road sport," says Francisco Valenzuela, a recreation program manager, based in Washington, D.C.[26] If you compare an appreciation of Nature from a speeding vehicle with the serenity of a solitary walk in the woods, you will begin to see that intimacy with Nature is in danger of being lost.

For the past decade, the number of visitors to our National Parks has been falling steadily. The National Park Service reports that between 1995 and 2005, Yosemite National Park suffered a twenty percent reduction in overnight stays and a twenty-four percent reduction in backcountry camping.[27] The situation was less severe at Yellowstone National Park, which reported an eight percent drop in visitors over the same period. Carlsbad Caverns National Park in southeast New Mexico suffered a whopping forty-five percent decline during the past two decades. Olympic National Park in Washington has lost one sixth of its visitors in just the past three years.[28]

Rising gas prices and increases in admission and lodging fees are being blamed for much of this decline, but there are other factors to be considered. With today's variety of vacation options, many young parents

---

Annual Reports of the NWF are available online: http://www.nwf.org/about/. Data on hunting and fishing licenses issued may also be obtained from the United States Fish & Wildlife Service, Department of the Interior. Online: http://www.fws.gov/news/historic/.

26. Mendoza, "National Forests Battle Trash, ATV's," para. 10.
27. Cart, "Camp outside? Um, no thanks!" para. 2.
28. Fish, "Old Faithful versus the Xbox," 104–5.

are choosing theme parks over national parks for outdoor entertainment. Baby boomers, who once thought nothing of camping out and sleeping on the hard ground, would now rather sleep in a comfy hotel bed after a glass of chardonnay and a gourmet dinner. Minorities do not visit the parks because they don't know much about them and fear that they are not safe places to be. It didn't help when Yosemite became the scene for the grisly murders of three women in February 1999.

A study published in the Journal of Environmental Management in 2006, which was funded by the National Science Foundation, pointed the finger at the use of electronics to explain falling attendance at the parks. The study scrutinized five common entertainment media variables—television, home movies, internet use, video games, and theater attendance. It concluded that the first four of these activities, combined with rising gasoline prices, accounted for 97.5 percent of the drop in park visitorship. The study stated, "We may be seeing evidence of a fundamental shift away from people's appreciation of Nature (biophilia, Wilson 1984) to 'videophilia,' which we here define as 'the new human tendency to focus on sedentary activities involving electronic media.'"[29]

Scott Gediman is a ranger who has worked at Yosemite National Park since 1996. He is also the Park's chief public information officer. Gediman is convinced that the steady decline in park attendance is largely due to kids having more entertainment options nowadays. "We certainly want parks to be relevant to young people today and to pass on the preservation ethic, but there is a different entertainment ethic. Half Dome is competing now with PlayStation and Xbox."[30] Gameworld Network, claiming to be one of the most popular online gaming destinations, while critical of Gediman's position, concedes, "there could be some truth to the notion that the more entertainment-centric kid's lives become, the less they go outside."[31]

In an effort to reach out to Americans born between 1980 and 2000, and to those who cannot make "real-time" visits, some parks are beginning to offer virtual tours. Glacier National Park currently provides *eHikes* for Internet users, with options that include day trips and even backpacking excursions. According to the *Saratogian*, New York's Saratoga National Historical Park is poised to jump from "muskets and three-cornered hats

---

29. Pergams and Zaradic, "Is love of Nature in the U.S." 393.
30. Manley, "Decline in Visitors Continues," para. 7.
31. Gameworld Network, "Decline in Visitors at Yosemite Blamed," para. 8.

to podcasting and streaming-video *eHikes*."[32] Visitors will soon be able to take advantage of downloadable *iPod* audio tours that they can listen to in the comfort of their automobiles. The Park's superintendent, Frank Dean, believes this will give Saratoga an edge in competing with Yellowstone and Yosemite for limited Federal funds.

I had an opportunity to meet with Scott Gediman in September 2007, to learn more about his efforts to stimulate interest in Yosemite, particularly with the newest generation of prospective visitors. One theme he hears over and over again from representatives of various groups is that "the parks need to be relevant." This places the leadership of the National Park Service on the "horns of a dilemma": Either they can fold their arms and hope that eventually more Generation X and Y's will show up at their gates, or they can make the parks more "relevant" by changing the way they are experienced. Such fundamental changes would likely involve the filtering of Nature through *iPods* and other electronic media. Unless revenues increase substantially, this will almost certainly necessitate funding cuts for traditional modes of park experience like camping, horseback riding, trail hikes, and real-time tours. Park officials could end up dressing the devil in a white dress and calling him "relevant." But in so-called relevant National Parks our young people would no longer connect with Nature in ways that could change their lives. Wilderness would be pushed ever deeper into the high country. School would be out!

LOVE FOR THE LAND

Along with the waning interest in outdoor recreation, there is evidence that many people in the western world no longer have a sense of connection to the sources of their food supply. Aldo Leopold warned, "There are two spiritual dangers in not owning a farm. One is the danger of supposing that breakfast comes from the grocery and the other that heat comes from the furnace."[33] At the turn of the last century, most Americans lived in rural areas and two in five lived on farms. But since then, millions of family-owned farms have been replaced by large scale industrial agricultural interests or by commercial and residential development.[34] One ominous report suggests that only thirty percent of the nation's 2.1 mil-

---

32. Kinney, "Park Hopes for Piece of Federal Funds," para. 1.
33. Leopold, *Sand County Almanac*, 6.
34. U.S. Department of Agriculture, *Agricultural Fact Book 2001–2002*, ch. 3.

lion remaining farms will pass to a second generation and less than ten percent will reach a third generation.[35]

Kentucky farmer, Wendell Berry, has become a leading advocate for a return to traditional agrarian culture and values. With more than thirty books to his credit, he is among the most distinguished of contemporary American authors. Berry believes that agribusiness and mechanization are largely responsible for our estrangement from the land, contributing to a serious deterioration of rural life. "Some prominent agricultural economists are still finding it possible to pretend that the only issues involved are economic, but that possibility is diminishing," Berry says. "I recently attended a meeting at which an agricultural economist argued that there is no essential difference between owning and renting a farm. A farmer stood up in the audience and replied: 'Professor, I don't think our ancestors came to America to *rent* a farm.'"[36] Clearly, there is a spiritual dimension to owning a piece of earth that yields sustenance for the rest of society. If current trends continue, however, it will not be long before less than one in one-hundred Americans will reside on farms, thus helping to insure that the deep affection we once held for the land will be little more than a faded memory.

NATURE'S EFFECTS ON CHILDREN

According to Richard Louv, a scholar in the field of child development, the lack of contact with Nature is having a decidedly negative effect on our children. In *Last Child in the Woods: Saving Our Children from Nature-Deficit Disorder*, Louv draws a clear link between Nature deprivation and obesity, Attention Deficit Disorder (ADD), and depression. He sheds light on a hypothesis by Edward O. Wilson, a leading scientist from Harvard University. In his hypothesis, identified as *biophilia*, Wilson asserts that humans have an innate "urge to affiliate with other forms of life."[37] Richard Louv's research supports Wilson's contention that an absence of this affiliation can have a detrimental long term impact on human beings.

Louv goes on to describe the intriguing new field of *ecopsychology*, as developed in the writings of Theodore Roszak.[38] In *Voice of the Earth*,

---

35. Spafford, "Legacy by Design," para. 8.
36. Berry, preface to *The Unsettling of America*.
37. Wilson, *Biophilia*, 1.
38. Roszak is credited with introducing the term *ecopsychology* into the vernacular

Roszak posits that the field of modern psychology has succeeded in dividing man's inner life from his external experience—that we have repressed our "ecological unconscious." The negative result of this repression, says Roszak, is an unhealthy separation from the evolutionary process. He proposes: "Once upon a time, all psychologies were 'ecopsychologies.' Those who sought to heal the soul took it for granted that human nature is densely imbedded in the world we share with animal, vegetable, mineral, and all the unseen powers of the cosmos."[39] Although the field of *ecopsychology* may not yet have gained a broad following, Roszak and Wilson could indeed be on to something.

I share in the growing concern over the eroding relationship between our children and the world of Nature. It is troubling to realize that many parents, in their well-meaning efforts to insulate their children from harm, have taught them irrational fears about what is "out there." Not long ago I took a trail walk with my little granddaughter along Trout Creek in Truckee, California. The creek meanders through an enticingly beautiful meadow, but the trail is narrow and the grass is as tall as a three-year old. After bounding along for a few steps, Rylie halted and urgently exclaimed, "Oh, snakes are here!" And then, "Bears!" I let her know that there was nothing to worry about: there were no snakes in the grass and the bears were friendly. Rylie's parents have encouraged her to explore the world around her and she has a healthy curiosity about her natural surroundings, so she trustingly accepted my explanation and we spent a memorable afternoon together. It is easy to see, however, how the wrong response might have turned a child's innate curiosity into unfounded concerns about the dangers posed by Nature's inhabitants.

Alexandra Picavet is the spokeswoman for Sequoia and Kings Canyon National Parks. She believes that our society is guilty of magnifying the normal fears that a child might have in wilderness settings like the national parks. "We scare them to death with signs and pamphlets warning them about bears, snakes, spiders, poison oak, drowning, driving on ice and in snow, and all the other disclaimers we provide," she says. "Small wonder they are terrified."[40]

---

in 1992. It has since become the accepted term for the study of the relationship between psychology and ecology.

39. Roszak, *Voice of the Earth*, 14.

40. Cart, "As Americans Change and Age," para. 16.

CHANGING TIMES

Many of us would agree that today's youth spend altogether too much time with computers, *iPods*, and all the rest of the gadgets of our digital age. "Baby boomers" had far fewer diversions when they were growing up. Neighborhood streets were central gathering places where boys and girls met to play ball, ride bikes, or just be together. I cannot remember the last time I saw a group of children playing ball on the quiet suburban street where I live.

For the youth of my generation, Nature was as close as the empty lot across the street. There were plenty of other wild places nearby, too, where a curious boy could stalk a cottontail, catch a lizard, or clutch a grasshopper. In our small town, just about every kid could bike to the lake, dig a few worms, and fish for bass and crappie. If the fish weren't biting, there were plenty of stickleback minnows and frogs to occupy a boy's time. The following story will illustrate just how close children were to Nature's doorstep in the not too distant past.

Our elementary school was bordered by a neglected old house on a vacated piece of land that had effectively reverted to a wilderness state. The place was a menagerie for all sorts of reptiles, rabbits, and other small critters that found the place much to their liking. One of my classmates, a boy named Chuck, was a notch or two different from the rest of the kids I knew. Like a real-life Dr. Doolittle, Chuck often drifted away from the school grounds and tended to the wild things on the adjacent property. One morning the sixth-grade teacher asked if any of the boys could catch a snake for observation by the science class. Everyone turned to Chuck, who enthusiastically volunteered. At lunchtime, he procured a large pickle jar from the cafeteria and disappeared into the neighboring jungle. In less than an hour he returned with eleven writhing gopher snakes. One can only imagine how he managed to get the lid on after that last snake had been crammed into the jar. At the teacher's nervous direction, Chuck soon released all but one back into the wild.

For today's suburban kids, access to places like vacant lots and nearby bass ponds is a rarity, and immediate exposure to Nature is far less common than it was for previous generations of young people. Parents have to be more intentional about getting their kids into the woods or even to the city park—we live in an era where the time demands of work and family are at the breaking point. What should be of grave concern to us all is that we have quite possibly raised the first generation of American children who, while they have had little or no experience in it, do not even have a basic curiosity about the world of Nature. Supporting this idea, Richard Louv tells of the boy who likes to play indoors, "cause that's where all the outlets are." It can safely be said that when our children's playtime is relegated to a 110-volt plug-in world, we will have surrendered much of what makes us uniquely human.

NATURE'S CREATIVE INFLUENCE

Louise Chawla is an environmental psychologist who has made some fascinating discoveries regarding childhood experience and the emergence of human creativity. In a study of the influence of Nature in the lives of five noted contemporary poets, Chawla discusses two prevalent theories of human behavior: First, she looks at the stimulus-response behaviorism espoused by B. F. Skinner,[41] "where responses established in childhood may condition lifelong patterns of preference and avoidance." Secondly, the empiricist model, "where lasting feelings for Nature derive from associations of fear or trust first learned in primary caregivers' hands."[42] In each of these modes of thinking, Nature has no intrinsic value, but is simply another of the multiple venues for human experience. While both of these theories are generally accepted in the field of practical psychology, neither is sufficient to account for the experiences that I have had in Nature. Nor do they do justice to the personal accounts that I have heard from countless others.

Chawla argues for an alternative in considering Nature's role in childhood development. She defers to William Wordsworth in proposing that the things in Nature may actually have value in and of themselves:

> the power of truth
> Coming in revelation, did converse
> With things that really are[43]

Chawla makes a compelling case for the validity of this "third way," suggesting that our experiences in the natural world not only stimulate hu-

---

41. B. F. Skinner (1904–90) was a Harvard psychologist, who pioneered research into human behaviorism and language development. Skinner concluded that all human and animal behavior is acquired and is patterned by reinforcement and conditioning.

42. Chawla, *In the First Country of Places*, 170.

43. Ibid., 170.

man creativity, but may actually help us make sense out of life. This theory seems highly plausible, particularly in light of the themes presented in this book.

Evidence for the creative influence of Nature is vividly displayed in the writings of C. S. Lewis (1898–1963). Lewis authored more than twenty books, including the hugely popular *Chronicles of Narnia*, which traces the journey of four English children who discover adventure in a mythical land behind a wardrobe closet in an old country house. Lewis lived his early years in Belfast, Ireland, when times were hard and opportunities were few. Finding an absence of beauty in the bleak world around him, he often retreated to an upstairs nursery, where his brother had fashioned a miniature garden on the lid of a biscuit tin. Lewis recalls the significance of his wilderness encounters in this upstairs hideaway:

> That was the first beauty I ever knew. What the real garden had failed to do, the toy garden did. It made me aware of Nature—not, indeed, as a storehouse of forms and colors, but as something dewy, fresh, exuberant. I do not think the impression was very important at the moment, but it soon became important in memory. As long as I live, my imagination of Paradise will retain something of my brother's toy garden.[44]

C. S. Lewis frequently returned in his imagination to this garden "Paradise" and tapped into a genius that has made him one of the most beloved of English writers. Lewis's contemporary and fellow Inkling,[45] J. R. R. Tolkein (1892–1973), is one of the literary giants of the modern age, having rendered such classics as *The Hobbit* (1937) and *Lord of the Rings* (1954–55). Unlike his friend, however, Tolkein was introduced to beauty in a more conventional fashion. As a youth, he received instruction in botany from his mother and he often explored the rustic English countryside, inspiring many of the dramatic scenes from his books. For both Lewis and Tolkein, the world of Nature was the cradle of their creative influence.

Beatrix Potter (1866–1943) spent her vacations at Hill Top Farm, the family's summer home in the Lakes District of rural northwest England. Often left alone by her busy parents, she began to write and illustrate children's books, producing dozens of magnificent tales about Peter Rabbit,

---

44. Lewis, *Surprised by Joy*, 7.

45. The Inklings was a group of men from Oxford University, who met regularly during the 1930s and 1940s to discuss literature and other academic topics.

Thomasina Tittlemouse, Jemima Puddleduck, and other garden guests with fascinating names. Later in her life, Potter, who vehemently opposed the development of small family farms, acquired the properties surrounding her estate. In her will she bequeathed more than 4,000 acres of rural land to the National Trust of England. It would be impossible to estimate just how much joy and laughter has been brought into children's lives by the effusive imagination and foresight of this exceptional woman.

In *The Sense of Wonder*, Rachel Carson warmly described her Nature experiences with a little boy named Roger on the Maine seacoast during the 1950s. She noted:

> A child's world is fresh and new and beautiful, full of wonder and excitement. It is our misfortune that for most of us that clear-eyed vision, that true instinct for what is beautiful and awe-inspiring, is dimmed and even lost before we reach adulthood. If I had influence with the good fairy who is supposed to preside over the christening of all children I should ask that her gift to each child in the world would be a sense of wonder.[46]

Carson deplored our "alienation from the sources of our strength," but saw in children an unspoiled sense of awe and an enthusiasm for Nature that could help sustain us well into our adult years.

Sometimes the wonder of a boyhood experience lodges itself deeply within our memory, providing an inspiration for the rest of our lives. Matt Bragg was introduced to the wilderness at an early age, often accompanying his father on hiking and camping trips throughout the eastern Sierras. On one memorable hike, Matt came upon a "golden fish" in a small mountain stream. His father explained that it was not the kind of fish that he would find in an aquarium, but was a golden trout—a rare and beautiful fish that few people ever see. The vision of the golden trout has remained in Matt's memory for more than thirty years. "I have never forgotten the golden fish," he says. "Though I never stopped to think about its significance, I just knew that I wanted to lead my life like that—wild and free." Experiences like Matt's are not uncommon. For some, the message is delivered in one golden moment of our youth. For others, it will come later as a subtle accumulation of knowledge, needing just the right timing and the proper setting to break through. If one spends enough time in the wilderness, these revelations are bound to occur.

---

46. Carson, *The Sense of Wonder*, 42–43.

SCIENCE AND THE WILDERNESS

With the rise of science and technology, Nature has become more accessible—and more vulnerable. Remote places that were once visited only by the most determined backpackers are now reachable by paved roads. Off-road vehicles have facilitated wilderness travel and sport utility vehicles (SUV's) now offer a luxury level of transportation. Rustic campsites have been replaced by hi-tech campgrounds that feature electricity, hot and cold running water, and flush toilets. Dehydrated food, high efficiency fuels, and developments in apparel and shelters have minimized human exposure to the natural elements. A century ago, lumbermen used unwieldy pump augurs, often taking several days to fell the largest trees. The invention of the chain saw, along with other modern lumbering techniques, has dramatically reduced the time needed to harvest a forest. Recent technological advances have enabled man to harness the power of wild rivers that were once unnavigable. With the advent of all-terrain vehicles (ATV's), helicopters, snowmobiles, and hydrofoils, there is virtually no place on earth that man cannot visit—and visit speedily.

But not everyone has endorsed unbridled technological progress and the complicity of science in the assault on Nature. One of the chief dissenters was Laurens van der Post, a native of South Africa and world traveler. After being imprisoned for three years during World War II, he spent the majority of his remaining years in search of the spirit of the African wilderness. By the time of his death in 1996, he had gained a considerable reputation as a leading critic of *apartheid*, and as a conservationist. Van der Post cautioned:

> Some of our scientists talk about "managing wilderness," and this worries me a bit. It is like saying they want to control revelation. But the moment you try to control it, there is no revelation. Not one of those scientists could have created the vision of something like wilderness. The vision of wilderness is not very complicated. We try to give it elaborate definitions, but we all know what wilderness really is, because we have it inside ourselves.[47]

When Rachel Carson released *Silent Spring* in 1962, she sent shock waves through the scientific community. The book opens as a fable set in an idyllic American town called Green Meadows. At first, all seems well in the little community, which is a desirable destination for sportsmen and

---

47. Meier, et al. *A Testament to the Wilderness*, 47.

vacationers. But as spring arrives, there is an eerie silence; there are no birds to sing, no trout to rise, or deer to hunt. All the animals are gone; every plant and tree and blade of grass has died from the effects of synthetic pesticides. Carson took a tremendous amount of criticism for the book, but she prevailed in exposing the collusion of corporations and government in suppressing the devastating effects of chemicals on the environment. Drawing on the support of conservation groups and influential friends, she convinced Congress to enact stringent legislation regarding the use of pesticides and other hazardous materials. Though reluctant at first, Rachel Carson became one of the world's leading environmentalists, leaving an enviable legacy of saving wildlife and generating concern for the preservation of wild places. In 1999, Carson was named by *Time* magazine as one of the twentieth century's one hundred most influential people. It is ironic that a few decades before, *Time* had criticized her for the "patently unsound" conclusions that she made in *Silent Spring*.

Loren Eiseley, anthropologist and writer, challenged scientific hubris in its inexorable quest for the "final brew or the ultimate chemical." Eiseley laments,

> If the day comes when the slime of the laboratory for the first time crawls under man's direction, we shall have great need for humbleness. As for me, if I am still around on that day, I intend to put on my old hat and climb over the wall as usual ... Somewhere among the seeds and beetle shells and abandoned grasshopper legs I find something that is not accounted for very clearly in the dissections to the ultimate virus or crystal or protein particle.[48]

Among Eiseley's writings is the intriguing tale of an encounter between a man and a muskrat on the brink of the disappearing wilderness. The story takes place on a busy lake, flush with the sounds of motor boats and screeching girls. Amid the washed-up beer cans along the water's edge, the man spies the shadowy figure of a young muskrat surfacing to nibble on the tender grasses growing there. Recognizing that the muskrat is not yet experienced enough to fear humans, the man warns him, "You had better run away now. You are in the wrong universe and must not make the same mistake again. I am really a very terrible and cunning beast. I can throw stones." With that the man harmlessly tosses a pebble in the direction of the muskrat. With a perplexed look, the little animal

---

48. Eiseley, *The Immense Journey*, 202, 208.

retreats and soon disappears into the lapping waves, taking with him "a world of sunlight."[49]

There is a profound sadness in contemplating the symbolism behind the story of the man and the muskrat. By our determined efforts to conquer the wilderness, we have effectively alienated ourselves from the natural world. In one of history's grim ironies—perhaps its grimmest irony—we have employed the special endowment of the human brain to develop powerful technologies that have ended up destroying most of the same wild places that we once called "home." In the words of Leo Marx, "the machine is in the garden,"[50] and things are never to be the same again. Yet, there remains a slim hope that the ancient wisdom of the indigenous people will somehow prevail, and that together with Chief Joseph, we will once again "hear voices in the depths of the forest." Nature still has much to tell us. But if we are to recover what we have lost, we must find trails leading back into the wilderness.

---

49. Eiseley, *The Firmament of Time*, 155–56.

50. For an examination of the pastoral idea in American culture, see Marx, *The Machine in the Garden*.

2

The Duckbuilder's Way

We do not have to risk the adventure alone;
for the heroes of all time have gone
before us. Where we had thought to be alone,
we shall be with all the world.

—Joseph Campbell

THE MASCULINE JOURNEY IS daunting. The path is often obscured by a tangled undergrowth of false signs and dead-end trails. A man can get bogged down by the demands of his multiple callings as a husband, a father, a son, and a provider. In the search for self and for a sense of direction, men can easily get blown off course. Many get lost in darkness and take a long time to get back on the trail. Some never find their way again. The journey is made more difficult by those who deny male uniqueness. Feminist activism, imbued with the values of the "sexual revolution" of the 1960s and 1970s, undermines the sublime differences between men and women. For their part, men have not fared well in coping with the blurred lines of traditional gender roles. In previous times men were the principal family breadwinners—the "hunters"—while women were the "gatherers." But as women entered the workforce to compete for jobs once reserved exclusively for men, the delicate tension between the sexes began to change. The premium once placed on men for their physical prowess has been largely negated in the exodus from rural to urban living.

Our society does not fathom the deep masculine heart. In recent decades we have resorted to drugging our children, especially boys, to better control what are often normal behaviors. Ritalin is a controversial central nervous system stimulant that is commonly prescribed for children with Attention Deficit Disorder (ADD) and Attention Deficit Hyperactivity Disorder (ADHD). Because of its similarities to cocaine and its potential for abuse, many doctors have labeled Ritalin, "a gateway drug." Estimates vary, but boys are several times more likely to receive Ritalin than girls. In an article, titled "Girls Get Extra School Help, While Boys Get Ritalin," *USA Today* hinted that, while there may not be a conspiracy against masculinity, there is evidence of a bias toward females in American education. Since boys and girls learn differently, the manner in which math and the sciences are presently being taught gives girls a built in advantage for academic success. *USA Today* warns, "Because schools are doing little to help boys adjust, males risk becoming second-class academic citizens."[1] Consider these startling facts from the *USA Today* article:

- Boys are four times more likely to be diagnosed with dyslexia than girls
- Boys receive Ritalin four to eight times the rate of girls
- Forty-four percent of girls are proficient in twelfth grade reading scores; only twenty-eight percent of boys
- Eighty-five percent of elementary teachers are women
- Females comprise fifty-six percent of college students

Classroom management is challenging for most teachers, especially when they must deal with active, noisy children. Primary school teachers will vouch for the fact that boys are typically louder, messier, and more aggressive than girls. While scientific research seems to indicate that boys are more prone to ADD and ADHD than girls, Ritalin and other stimulants are probably administered far too liberally to suppress hyperactivity. Take the case of Chris Kaman, center for the Los Angeles Clippers basketball team. In 2008, Kaman revealed to the *Los Angeles Times* that he was diagnosed with ADHD when he was just two years old and he began taking Ritalin. Hope139, a research organization that studies the brain,

---

1. *USA Today*, "Girls Get Extra School Help," para. 4–12.

recently discovered that Kaman was misdiagnosed, along with as many as fifteen percent of other kids with ADHD.[2] Meanwhile, Kaman has been the victim of serious side effects from the drug, truncating his chances for leading a normal life. He is now undergoing a promising new treatment called "neuro-feedback," which reads brainwave activity to reinforce calm thoughts and reduce over-stimulation to the brain.

To account for the behavioral variances between the sexes, psychologists once thought that boys' brains were slower in developing than girls'. But experts now believe that male and female brains develop in a different sequence. The right side of the male brain (related to visual memory and spatial relationships) tends to develop more quickly than the left (related to language and speech); girls tend to use both at an early stage. Boys have an edge in solving abstract problems, while girls are better listeners and are inclined to take in more sensory data than boys. Male toddlers tend to walk and talk later than females.[3] The presence of the male sex hormone, called testosterone, accounts for increased activity and aggressiveness in boys, who are less sensitive to physical sensation and have a harder time surviving infancy, with a mortality rate that is much higher than that of girls.[4] Although we know that boys are hardwired differently from their opposite sex, we may not yet fully understand the nuances of male childhood development.

Exposure to calm soothing environments is helpful for everyone, particularly for children with learning disabilities and hyperactivity. Gary Porter, an educator from New York, and his wife, Beth, have two sons who were diagnosed with ADHD early in their childhood. Thanks to active intervention by their parents and clinical professionals, the boys, Gary John and Frank, have been able to overcome the effects of hyperactivity. Interestingly, Beth and Gary have a slightly different take on what factors were most important. While they both concede that structure and the setting of explicit boundaries for behavior were critical components, Gary believes strongly that his sons' experience with the Boy Scouts was also

---

2. Abrams, "Kaman recalls childhood frustrations," D4.

3. Data on male and female development is taken from Men's Health Network (MHN), a not-for-profit educational network, committed to improving men's health through education. Online: http://www.menshealthnetwork.org.

4. U.S. Department of Health & Human Services, Center for Disease Control and Prevention, *National Vital Statistics Reports* 53, no. 15, p. 3.

pivotal. "ADHD compromised the boys' ability to interact effectively with their peers," Gary notes.

> We live in a digital age where a boy is measured by his skill level with computers and video games. Take him into the woods and you step away from all that. In the world of Nature, everyone is on the same footing. Through scouting, the wilderness became a place where Gary John and Frank could create their own successes and build their self-confidence. The real competition is the competition with yourself; being better than you were the day before.

As scouts, the boys learned to pitch tents, tie knots, and build fires. They also learned that Nature is "the place of raw power."

THE DISAPPEARING MALE

In today's "virtual world," kids are far more likely to spend time tapping a keyboard than turning the pages of a novel. Apparently boys have been affected more severely than girls by the trend away from reading. Children who are read to regularly by an adult tend to become readers themselves and, as any teacher will tell you, reading accelerates learning and fosters creativity. Judith Kleinfeld, distinguished researcher from the University of Alaska in Anchorage, cites an important 2002 study that showed that twenty-three percent of sons of white college-educated parents were "below basic" on standardized tests—a seventy-six percent increase over what it had been a decade earlier! By comparison, the same study showed that only six percent of girls fell below the basic reading proficiency line.[5] Encouraging literacy is the obligation of both teachers and parents. I wonder if fathers are sharing equitably in the responsibility of reading to their kids.

The gender gap in the teaching profession does not help alleviate a serious and growing problem for boys—lack of early contact with positive male role models. There are simply far too few men in America's classrooms. Elementary education has always been a bastion for women teachers, but the number of their male counterparts has been slipping steadily since the 1960s. According to the National Teachers Association (NEA), men now comprise only nine percent of elementary school teachers.[6] Regardless of the reasons for this disturbing trend, boys too seldom

5. Britt, "Why Johnny Can't Read," line 19.
6. National Education Association, "Are Male Teachers on the Road to Extinction?"

experience the influential presence of exemplary male leaders in learning environments during their foundational years. By the time an "at-risk" boy reaches adolescence and puberty, it is often too late to curb his tendencies toward destructive choices like drug abuse, gang association, dropping out of school, and criminal activity.

The dearth of principled male leadership has had a crippling effect on masculinity and on society at large. With contemporary lifestyle options, flexible living arrangements, and ease of divorce, too many men opt out of their domestic responsibilities. Since the 1960s, the birthrate to unmarried parents has risen markedly, and now fewer households than ever before are headed by males. Based on 2000 U.S. Census data, more than one-third of children are now born to unwed parents.[7] Among minorities, conditions are especially deplorable. According to the census, births to unmarried black women had risen to sixty-eight percent; among Hispanics to 43.5 percent. Where are the men who father our children?

In the absence of dutiful fathers, young men turn to their peers for validation, often leading to calamitous results. Gang shootings, drug trafficking, and tagging have not only blighted our communities, but have eroded the self respect of our youth. Men are four times more likely to commit suicide than women, and homicide consistently ranks among the leading causes of death for American males—especially minorities—younger than thirty years of age.[8] Under the guise of "body art," piercings and tattoos all too often serve as outward manifestations of deep inner conflicts affecting young adults.

Men, who outnumber women by a ratio of fifteen to one, overwhelmingly populate our prisons. Approximately one of every seventy-five adult men in the U.S. is behind bars.[9] The situation is acutely severe for racial minorities, who in 2004 comprised sixty-one percent of prison and jail inmates. One in eight black men in their late twenties was in jail or prison, as were 3.6 percent of Hispanic men. By comparison, less than two percent of white men in that age group were under incarceration.[10]

---

para. 4.

[7]. U.S. Department of Health & Human Services, Center for Disease Control and Prevention, *National Vital Statistics Reports* 52, no. 10, p. 57.

[8]. U.S. Department of Health & Human Services, Center for Disease Control and Prevention, *National Vital Statistics Reports* 55, no. 19, p. 7–10.

[9]. Cass, "One of Every 75 U.S. Men in Prison," line 1.

[10]. U.S. Department of Justice, Office of Justice Programs, *Bureau of Justice Statistics*

The phenomenon of the disappearing male is amplified by a television commercial that aired at the start of the 2007 football season. The ad was sponsored by the National Football League (NFL), and it featured quarterback Vince Young, one of professional sports' brightest new stars. As the camera pans in, Young begins, "A lot of people really don't like the tattoo thing, but ..." He then points to his tattoos and explains that each one signifies his relationship with the most important people in his life. He mentions no less than eight individuals for whom he has, or will have, a tattoo. None of them are men.

The western world is clearly in the throes of an epidemic of lost male identities and it seems like fewer and fewer of us are capable of doing anything about it. One person who is making an effort is Bill Doulos. Bill is the director of Jubilee Enterprises, a transitional housing project based in San Gabriel, California. Jubilee provides shelter and vocational training for hundreds of recovering addicts and alcoholics, eighty percent of whom are men. Bill has worked with society's rejects and down-and-outs for so long that he "lost count long ago" of the number of men and women that he has tried to help. He gifted the deeds to each of Jubilee's four homes, which serve as waypoints for recovering addicts who are trying to put their fractured lives back together.

Bill Doulos well understands the destructive forces of addiction, for he too is a recovering alcoholic. And while he is familiar with the dark reaches of a man's inner wilderness, Bill did not have his first meaningful Nature experience until late in his life. He relates this exceptional story:

> About six years ago I developed a passion for picking up golf balls down around the local golf course. This grew out of my need for some walking exercise to improve my health, but I needed additional motivation, so I found myself searching for lost golf balls along the wooded path at the wash that runs down the middle of the course. As a child I had seldom strayed off the beaten path, so this was an adventure in itself. One day I went down to my customary spot after a January rain and I noticed that the stream had a lot more water in it than usual. Undeterred, I waded in to plant myself in front of a cascading golf ball to scoop it up. But I greatly underestimated the force of the water flow and as I stepped into the stream I was quickly swept off my feet. I couldn't believe the rush of the water and it gave me a psychic rush as well. I was aware that up ahead there was a drop-off that seemed gentle enough in

---

NCJ 198272, 3–11.

ordinary times, but this was no ordinary time. Finally, I caught hold of something and I pulled myself out of the water. I was wobbly on my feet for quite some time. I suppose I had floated for a couple hundred yards, feeling very helpless in the grip of Mother Nature and very relieved to have emerged unscathed. This experience brought a taste of wet adventure to an otherwise barren life. I wish I could taste it again without the risk, but without the risk, where would the sense of adventure be? For a brief moment I saw myself as a 'wild man.' I was dangerous.

No one who knows Bill would say that he has led a barren life, yet it took him nearly sixty years of living to "stray off the beaten path"—to experience the sense of adventure that he was meant for. There is wildness in every man's heart that can take time to surface. Like Iron John, we may have a spell cast on us that is lifted only by an experience in Nature. Later in this book, we will hear the stories of several men and women who, like Bill Doulos, became believers in the magic of the wilderness.

THE QUEST FOR BEAUTY

Why is Nature such an effective communicator? Think for a moment: Have you ever heard of someone spending hundreds of dollars for a *Vision Quest* at the summit of the Empire State Building, or of someone who wrote great poetry while pondering the meaning of a cell tower disguised to look like a tree? Of course not! There is a purity in Nature—an unspoiled essence—that is not duplicated by skyscrapers or multi-level freeway interchanges. Human fabrications cannot compare with the simple elegance of Nature's creations. As a great teacher once proffered, "Consider the lilies of the field ... not even King Solomon in all his glory was arrayed like one of these."[11]

Nature appeals to our senses in ways that other stimuli cannot. She displays a dazzling assortment of colors, shapes, sizes, and composition. Nature can be fragrant, sometimes pungent. She is soft and supple, brittle and unyielding; warm and inviting one moment, then cold and forbidding the next. Skies may be blue, or they may be angry shades of gray. Nature is magnificent! Nature is beautiful! It is this beauty that draws us in.

There are few places that display Nature's beauty more resplendently than the Yosemite Valley, about which there are many references in this

---

11. Matt 6:28–29.

book. These references are not coincidental. Since it was first written about in the 1850s, Yosemite has been particularly influential in our understanding of wilderness. With its towering waterfalls, imposing granite cliffs, and verdant meadows, Yosemite offers some of the most extravagant natural scenery on the planet. No less an authority than Ralph Waldo Emerson once noted that Yosemite was "the only place that came up to the brag!"[12] Even after a particularly strenuous day in the saddle, famous American journalist Horace Greeley was wont to concede, "There is no single wonder of Nature on earth which can claim superiority over the Yosemite."[13]

The first person to recognize the enormous tourist potential of Yosemite was James M. Hutchings. Hutchings took one of the earliest recorded sightseeing parties into the valley in June 1855. Later, he operated one of its original hotels and became a tireless promoter of Yosemite's natural attractions. In 1886 he released *In the Heart of the Sierras*, which is still regarded as one of the best records of the early history of Yosemite. The book contains many stirring personal accounts of Yosemite's glories, written by those fortunate few who had the means to travel there. Here is what some of those early visitors had to say when the Yosemite Valley first came into view:

> Nature has here lifted her curtain to reveal the vast and the infinite. It elicited no adjectives, no exclamations. With a bewildering sense of divine power and human littleness, I could only gaze in silence till the view strained my brain and pained my eyes, compelling me to turn away and rest from its oppressive magnitude.
>
> I may as well try to measure a rainbow with a two-foot rule, as to take this in.
>
> The overpowering sense of the sublime, of awful desolation, of transcendent marvelousness and unexpectedness, that swept over us, as we reined our horses sharply out of green forests and stood upon a high jutting rock that overlooked this rolling, upheaving sea of granite mountains, holding, far down in its rough lap, the vale of meadow and grove and river—such a tide of feeling, such stoppage of ordinary emotions, comes at rare intervals in any life.
>
> I was never so near heaven in all my life.[14]

---

12. Hutchings, *In the Heart of the Sierras*, 10.
13. Russell, *One Hundred Years in Yosemite*, 72.
14. Hutchings, *In the Heart of the Sierras*, 14–15, 17–18.

There is a certain reverence in the opulent wording of these Victorian writers that only serves to intensify the images they portray. Contemporary writers, while using differing language, recount their impressions of Yosemite with much the same feelings of awe and wonderment. Regardless of one's vocabulary, it is evident that the beauty of Nature, as displayed in places like Yosemite National Park, can make a profound impact on us.

HOW NATURE TEACHES

Nature teaches *evocatively*, rather than *provocatively*. Provocation stirs one to action and implies stimulation. Evocation draws out emotion, implying reflection, even contemplation. Provocation does not ask for permission and needs a response for validation. Evocation, on the other hand, waits for an open heart and mind and needs no validation. Truth often surfaces in evocative environments.

While Nature is a patient teacher, she is by no means a passive one. On the contrary, when you consider natural disasters like earthquakes, floods, hurricanes, and tsunamis, Nature can appear to be capricious and aggressive. The natural world is often depicted as a battleground between the dualistic forces of good and evil, light and darkness, warmth and cold. But life is not easy, and there are no simple answers to Nature's mysteries. The fact remains that the lessons of the wild are taught very subtly; it is when our hearts and minds are receptive to learning that the gift of wisdom presents itself. When we are in zones of deep acuity we are in what has been called "liminal space."

Liminal space defines an area of our lives, inward or outward, where we are most vulnerable to learning. It is found on the margins of our experience—in the difficult times of transition, like the loss of a job, the death of a spouse, or in the realization that one's dream was only an illusion. Liminal space is created when an addict hits rock bottom, or when a man finally accepts the inevitability of his demise. Richard Rohr calls liminal space, "the ultimate teachable space. In some sense, it is the only teachable space."[15] Liminal space usually develops in our interiors, but as we have already seen, the physical world of Nature offers plenty of teachable space, too.

---

15. Rohr, *Adam's Return*, 135. According to Rohr, the concept of liminal space was refined by Victor Turner in *The Ritual Process*.

SYMBOL OF THE WILDERNESS

Nothing so symbolizes Nature as a tree. Fondly etched in the memory of my childhood is this simple, elegant poem:

> *I think that I shall never see*
> *A poem lovely as a tree*
>
> *A tree whose hungry mouth is prest*
> *Against the sweet earth's flowing breast*
>
> *A tree that looks at God all day*
> *And lifts her leafy arms to pray*
>
> *A tree that may in summer wear*
> *A nest of robins in her hair;*
>
> *Upon whose bosom snow has lain*
> *Who intimately lives with rain.*
>
> *Poems are made by fools like me*
> *But only God can make a tree.*[16]

    Joyce Kilmer wrote the words during the winter of 1913, as he looked out over a grove of trees from an upstairs window in his parents' New Jersey home. One cannot escape the deep humility and reverence for Nature that burst forth from the poet's soul in that liminal moment.

    Of all the trees I know, my favorite is the oak, especially those that dot the landscape along the sprawling hills of inland California. These stalwarts grow like living monuments, with grace and a sense of perfect proportion that will never be captured on an artist's canvas, or by a poet's rhyme. Oak trees have wrinkled skin and wide, wavy arms, which can extend out more than fifty feet. They emit an intensely masculine fragrance, and while they may have rugged exteriors, oak trees have tender hearts. In weariness, I have rested against their trunks and slept beneath their shaded canopies. Although some of the oaks I have met are ancient, their wisdom is not measured by the passing of years.

    Shel Silverstein's classic allegory, *The Giving Tree*, tells of a tree that loves a small boy. Little by little, the tree gives all that it is made of—its fruit, its leaves, its branches—to help his friend. As the story draws to an end, the boy, who is by now a tired old man, returns to the tree and confesses that there is not much else that he needs. Although it is has been reduced to nothing but a stump, the tree has more yet to give and it calls

---

16. Kilmer, *Trees and Other Poems*, 7.

out to him, "'Come, Boy, sit down. Sit down and rest.' And the tree was happy."[17] One of the marvelous aspects of this story is that the tree never sees his lifelong friend as anyone other than a child. It looks beyond the old man's wearied look to a vision of innocence that was once a little boy. There is a deep meaning behind the presence of a tree.

Viktor Frankl was taken prisoner by the Nazi's during World War II. He entered Auschwitz as a strict determinist, but stripped naked and utterly humiliated, he came to the profound realization that he still possessed the inner freedom to choose his response to the cruelties being inflicted by his captors on him and his fellow inmates. Frankl relates the chilling story of an extraordinary encounter he had in a German concentration camp. As both a medical doctor and a psychiatrist, he was often called upon to attend to the sick and dying. On this occasion he visited the cell of a young woman, who was thought to be mentally ill. Frankl found out otherwise. In the course of their conversation the woman pointed to the branch of a chestnut tree that was barely visible through a small window in her cell. The branch held two fragile blossoms on its stems. She explained to Frankl, "This tree here is the only friend I have in my loneliness. I often talk to this tree." Taken by surprise, he asked her if the tree ever responded. When the woman answered affirmatively, he anxiously asked her what the tree said. She peacefully replied, "It said to me, 'I am here—I am here—I am life, eternal life.'"[18]

The woman's wilderness had been reduced to a single tree. Oh, but what a tree! The solitude and the silence of her suffering had prepared her to hear the voices of eternity being gently spoken through its quivering branches. She extracted every ounce of joy and wisdom from the singular thing of beauty that stood steadfastly beyond her prison walls. How much more should we be grateful for the experience that awaits us in a forest full of trees!

Viktor Frankl miraculously survived his harrowing ordeal. Countless times, through a veil of tears, I have read the following account of his reintroduction to Nature:

> One day, a few days after the liberation, I walked through the country past flowering meadows, for miles and miles, toward the market town near the camp. Larks rose to the sky and I could hear

---

17. Silverstein, *The Giving Tree*, n.p.
18. Frankl, *Man's Search for Meaning*, 77–78.

their joyous song. There was no one to be seen for miles around; there was nothing but the wide earth and sky and the larks' jubilation and the freedom of space. I stopped, looked around and up to the sky—and then went down on my knees. At that moment there was very little I knew of myself or of the world—I had but one sentence in mind—always the same: 'I called to the Lord from my narrow prison and He answered me in the freedom of space.'[19]

Men must sometimes learn the lessons of the wild amidst horrific circumstances. But then—in solitude and in freedom—when confronted anew by Nature's ageless beauty, they have an experience that eludes all description.

When I think of the Holocaust, I am struck by the intense feelings of despair and loneliness that the captives must have felt. As most men are, I am fearful of being alone. I am, like you, a "social animal" who is drawn to the company of other men and women. Community sustains us and validates us as belonging to something bigger than ourselves. Our lives are made more meaningful by the work that we do, the families that we nurture, the charities that we support, the organizations to which we belong, and the churches where we worship. Like the woman in Frankl's story, we seek companionship—even the companionship of a tree—and a circle of friends. We cleave to our spouse and our close relations to support and sustain us as we grow older. When a family member dies we convene to remember the deceased and renew our family ties. But it becomes abundantly clear as life goes on, and as our generation begins to pass away, that these ties are knitted amongst fewer and fewer of our closest kin. Our parents may have died, or perhaps we have lost a sibling or our wife or husband. Despite its repression, instinct tells us that our exit from planet Earth, like our entrance, will be solitary. This is entirely too much aloneness for most men.

If we dread loneliness, why do so many of us seek the remoteness of the woods to hike, hunt, fish, or just to be counted present? Perhaps it is our desperate search for meaning and a sense of direction for our lives that beckons us into the wild. Many men put their searches on hold, sometimes for years. Others do not admit their innermost longings and never take the first step. But a few men I know are actively tracking their authentic selfhood; trying to uncover who they truly are and what compass point they ought to follow. These men are prime candidates to learn

---

19. Ibid., 96.

Nature's lessons—men whose lives can be changed by their experiences in the wild and in other liminal places.

Thoreau once noted, "Many men fish all their lives and never know it's not fish they're after."[20] As men, we seldom pause to ask ourselves why we are so attracted to Nature—why the wilderness has such a powerful magnetism. Is it possible that inside each one of us is the subconscious realization that our true heart lies at the bottom of a lake (remember Iron John) or at the top of a mountain or in the depths of the forest? I believe that it is not only possible, but that it is undeniable!

DISCOVERING DUCKS

Whether on a backpacking trip or a *Vision Quest*, it is vital that men recognize the signs along the trail. For eons, experienced hikers, horsemen, and explorers have placed piles of rocks, called "ducks," at trailheads and along routes of travel. Ducks are usually made with a few small stones, but can be larger, depending on what's available. Although no one is sure about the origins of this ancient practice, it is clear that ducks serve important purposes. Like the trail of pebbles in the forest of the old Germanic fairy tale of Hansel and Gretel, hikers use ducks to retrace their steps and find their way back again. Ducks also serve as markers for those who will come along later. A trail can also be marked by what is called a "blaze"—hence the name, "trailblazer." A blaze is made by cutting out a small section of bark from a tree at a point high enough to be visible even in the deepest snows. The presence of a duck or a blaze is a sure sign that you are on the trail.

If you have ever felt the sense of desperation at being lost, then you also know the enormous relief that accompanied your rediscovery of the way home. If you happened upon a duck or a blaze, you would have felt an abiding sense of gratitude to the anonymous person who put it there. Quaker philosopher, D. Elton Trueblood, once observed: "A man has made at least a start on discovering the meaning of human life when he plants shade trees under which he knows full well he will never sit."[21]

In American lore there is a persistent tale of just such a man—a mythical character named "Johnny Appleseed," who is credited with planting mil-

---

20. The Thoreau Institute at Walden Woods Library, "Thoreau's Life and Writings," line 4.

21. Trueblood (1900–1994), Earlham College philosophy professor, was an advisor to several American presidents, including Herbert H. Hoover, Richard M. Nixon, and Dwight D. Eisenhower. See James R. Newby, ed. *Elton Trueblood*.

lions of apple trees throughout Illinois, Indiana, and Ohio. But Johnny was more than fictional. His real name was John Chapman (1774–1847) and he traveled extensively, planting trees and orchards wherever he went. While it is difficult to determine where the man ended and the legend began, Johnny Appleseed became a folk hero and his gravesite in Fort Wayne, Indiana's Archer Park has been designated a national historic landmark.

Duckbuilders and tree planters are cut from the same bolt of cloth. They are givers, providing a benchmark and a sense of security for those who follow in their footsteps. While we will seldom have an opportunity to personally thank a duckbuilder, when we find their trail markers we form an invisible bond with them. Learning more about duckbuilders can add to our understanding of wilderness; learning to become a duckbuilder can alter the course of our lives, and thereby change the world.

LEGACY OF WILDERNESS HEROES

Who were the duckbuilders and what drove them into the wilderness? Why did they leave such obvious signs along the way? Duckbuilders come from every station and walk of life. Some of them have already been mentioned in this book, but there are countless others: religious leaders, scientists, artists, writers, inventors, explorers, sailors, fishermen, teachers, and artisans—each of whom took enormous risks to see what lay beyond the frontiers of human experience. Here are some of their stories.

A most unlikely duckbuilder was a sixteenth century Polish cleric named Nicolaus Copernicus (1473–1543), who became entranced by the wilderness of the heavens. After a lifetime of diligent observation, he arrived at the then revolutionary conclusion that the Earth revolves around the sun. The notion of a *heliocentric* solar system flew in the face of the long accepted earth-centered cosmology, which originated with Aristotle (384–322 B.C.) and was refined by Ptolemy in the second century A.D. Powerful Roman Catholic leaders so vilified Copernicus for his heretical hypothesis that his findings did not appear in print until he lay on his deathbed. However, his book, entitled *De revoutionibus*, became ducks for another bold adventurer, whose name was Galileo Galilei.

Galileo (1564–1642), a brilliant Italian scientist and inventor, was fascinated by Copernicus' findings. In 1609 he began work on the first telescope, which he later used to demonstrate that his predecessor had correctly understood our solar system. Like Copernicus, Galileo was scorned by Church officials. He was brought before the Holy Office of the Inquisition, where he was tried and convicted of heresy. To avoid possible execution, he was forced to sign a confession and sentenced to confinement in the Tuscan embassy in Rome. Suffering from chronic illness and impaired vision, Galileo spent much of his time in the embassy's gardens, confiding in his daughter that without his interludes in the outdoors he could not have endured his persecutions. Inspired by the fecundity of Nature, he once wrote a popular parable of the song of the cicada fly. Ironically, this was one of the favorite poems of Pope Urban VIII, who was one of Galileo's chief persecutors.[22] Galileo was ultimately vindicated and is considered one of the founding fathers of modern science. One does not have to be a scientist, however, to recognize him as one of the duckbuilders.

If integrity be the judge, Albert Schweitzer (1875–1965) lived one of the most distinguished lives on record. The son of a German pastor, Schweitzer was deeply affected by a series of childhood Nature experiences, instilling in him a "reverence for life" that was to mark the course of his unusual journey. When he was thirty-eight years old he traveled to the African Congo, abandoning several profitable career interests as a physician, teacher, and musician. Branded as an enemy by the French provincial authorities, he was still permitted to practice medicine. Most of the natives had never seen a white man, but Schweitzer and his wife, Helene, soon earned their trust. Albert Schweitzer was on a quest, but the reasons why were still shrouded in mystery when he and Helene arrived in equatorial Africa in the spring of 1913. While he felt compelled to atone for the "terrible crimes we read about in the newspapers," Schweitzer was aware of something else drawing him into the jungle. Then a revelation came his way:

> Late on the third day, at the very moment, when at sunset, we were making our way through a herd of hippopotamuses, there flashed upon my mind, unforeseen and unsought, the phrase, "Reverence for Life." The iron door yielded; the path in the thicket had become visible.[23]

Albert Schweitzer had seen a vision in the wilderness. At the outbreak of World War I in 1914, he and Helene were repatriated to France as civilian

22. Sobel, *Galileo's Daughter*, 114–15, 150, 159, 214, 237.
23. Free, ed. *Animals, Nature and Albert Schweitzer*, 22.

interns. A prolonged illness prevented Albert from returning to Africa until ten years later, at which time he began establishment of the first permanent hospital facility at Lambarene in the central African rainforest. Though he spent most of his days in isolation, his lifetime of selfless service did not go unnoticed by the world community. In 1952, he was chosen to receive the Nobel Peace Prize for his humanitarian efforts, driven by his compassion for all living things. It is not surprising that when many of the world's leading conservationists followed in Schweitzer's footsteps, they found his ducks along the trail. Rachel Carson, who dedicated *Silent Spring* to his memory, was one.

THE AMERICAN TRAILBLAZER

In America we boast our own unique assemblage of colorful characters who blazed the trails into Nature's wilderness. Legends like Meriwether Lewis, William Clark, Jedidiah Smith, Kit Carson, John C. Fremont, Buffalo Bill Cody, and Theodore Roosevelt were lured by the promise of adventure to the American frontier before it passed into the pages of history. Less well known, but no less adventuresome was Norman Clyde—arguably the greatest American mountain climber of the twentieth century. The mountains were Clyde's adopted home and he was legendary for toting hundred pound backpacks loaded with heavy pots and pans, multiple cameras, fishing rods and reels, a pair of revolvers, and a small library of books written in five languages. He logged thousands of miles on alpine trails and achieved nearly one hundred "first ascents" in the Sierra Nevada's—an astounding thirty-five of them during 1925 and 1926. With more than 600 successful climbs, he ranks among the most prolific mountaineers on record. Jules Eichorn, Clyde's frequent climbing companion, reminisces about the "Old Gaffer": "There can never be another human being so completely in tune with his environment—the mountains—as Norman Clyde."[24]

Clyde's predecessor was a duckbuilder named George G. Anderson, who in October 1875 became the first human to stand atop Half Dome in Yosemite National Park. Within a few days, several others (including the first woman) had used his cleverly devised rope ladder to replicate Anderson's climb—a feat considered impossible up until that time. Among those early climbers was a man by the name of John Muir.

24. Clyde, from the prologue to *Norman Clyde of the Sierra Nevadas*.

Muir had come with his father from Scotland to Fountain Lake, Wisconsin in 1849, when he was eleven years old. His father was a strict disciplinarian who demanded long hours of hard labor on the farm and "spared not the rod" on his precocious son. Despite his father's stern warnings against reading books, save for the Bible, young John became a voracious reader. He and his younger brother, David, spent most of their precious free time in the woods and fields that encircled the farm. Amidst an abundance of flora and fauna, the Muir boys acquired a deep affection for the natural world. John recounts those early days:

> This sudden plash into pure wildness—Baptism in Nature's warm heart—how utterly happy it made us. Nature streaming into us, wooingly teaching her wonderful growing lessons . . . every wild lesson a love lesson, not whipped, but charmed into us. Oh, that glorious Wisconsin wilderness![25]

Muir left Wisconsin when he was twenty-five, beginning an unparalleled period of travel throughout the Americas. By the time he made his way to California in the spring of 1868, he was well regarded as an inventor and a machinist, but it was his keen interest in botany that had brought him westward in hopes of finding virgin wilderness where he could study trees and plants and record his findings for the scientific community.

After a few restless days in the bustling city of San Francisco, Muir inquired of a gentleman who was passing by as to "the nearest way out of town to the unsettled part of the State." When asked where he wanted to go, Muir replied, "Anywhere that's wild!"[26] Muir had heard stories of the pristine beauty of Yosemite, so at the stranger's suggestion he quickly set off on foot to see it for himself. The trek of a few hundred miles was nothing more than a leisurely "tramp" for the slim Scotsman, whose epic journey from Kentucky to Florida is well-chronicled in his *Thousand Mile Walk to the Gulf*. As he made his way eastward, Muir meticulously recorded his observations of the grand scenery of California. He is credited with providing the first detailed account of the florid San Joaquin Valley, while standing on the rim of Pacheco Pass. It was from this vantage point

---

25. Bade, ed. *The Life and Letters of John Muir*, 1.39.

26. Sargent, *John Muir in Yosemite*, 9. Note: Sargent borrowed the account of Muir's arrival in San Francisco and travel to Yosemite from the original story, first published in a magazine called *Old and New* in 1872.

that Muir first gazed on the snow-crested Sierra Nevada Mountains and inspired by their grandeur, aptly named them the "Range of Light."

Muir soon made his way into the Yosemite Valley, where he spent several eventful days, vowing to return and explore the region more thoroughly as time and finances would permit. The following spring he found employment with a sheepherder named Delaney, who was driving his flocks to Yosemite. In the company of these "hoofed locusts," Muir again arrived in the valley, where he stayed for the rest of the summer, exploring nearly every step of it. With the early onset of winter, Muir reluctantly left, "... praying and hoping that Heaven will shove me back again." He did not have long to wait. After a few weeks of mending fences and breaking horses on the Delaney Ranch, he grew restless and headed back to Yosemite on foot. In a letter to a friend, Muir pined: "I must return to the mountains—to Yosemite ... I am bewitched, enchanted and tomorrow I must start for the great temple to listen to the winter songs and sermons preached and sung only there."[27]

It was during those rapturous days of 1869 that John Muir penned some of the most intimate descriptions of Nature ever written. His keen observations of the geology of the Yosemite area were published in several prominent journals and he soon earned recognition as a geologist as well as a botanist. Muir discovered hundreds of "living glaciers" and found evidence that the Yosemite Valley had been formed by glacial action. This contradicted the popularly accepted view, championed by one of America's leading scientists, Josiah D. Whitney. Whitney headed up the California Geological Survey and he claimed that the valley could only have been formed by a cataclysmic collapse of the Earth's crust. The controversy was short-lived however, as Muir's hypothesis soon received near unanimous support among America's scientific elite.

John Muir is closely associated with the establishment of Yosemite National Park in 1890, and was installed as the first president of the Sierra Club two years later. Along with John Burroughs, he was probably the most recognized Nature writer of his day. Muir was among the most vocal critics of the damming of the Hetch Hetchy Valley, to which he affectionately referred as his "other Yosemite." In 1914, in ill health and exhausted over the bitter Hetch Hetchy defeat, he died in Los Angeles on Christmas Eve, at the age of seventy-six. Seventy years later, the *San Francisco Chronicle*

---

27. Bade, ed. *The Life and Letters of John Muir*, 1.202.

cited that John Muir had been voted by the California Historical Society as the single most important person in the history of California.[28]

Trailblazers like Albert Schweitzer and John Muir possess admirable traits, such as courage, confidence, and determination. But there is more. They respond affirmatively to an inner calling and thereby elevate the human condition. There are several important reasons to carefully consider our own journeys in light of their example:

- To gauge the power of Nature in adding to our awareness of our world and to expand our existential knowledge of ourselves, as human beings
- To challenge our paradigms, testing whether our views of life and people can hold up under scrutiny
- To see that there are lessons to be learned in the natural world, and examine whether or not a wilderness experience can be applied to life's situations back in the "civilized" world
- To develop a compelling vision for our lives
- To continue to nurture a "reverence for life," supporting the essential work of conservation and the restoration of wild places for the benefit of ours and future generations

THE PRIMARY LESSON

Unlike Bill Doulos, whose story was told earlier, I was taught my first wilderness lesson when I was very young. The instruction took place in my grandparents' vegetable garden sometime during my second year. The garden took up a good portion of the backyard and was planted in a myriad of squashes, carrots, and tomatoes. It had been carefully cultivated by my grandfather, who was a farmer before moving to the city. "Pop" had designed a simple irrigation system, fed by a single hose placed strategically at the end of the rows. My grandmother, who was babysitting me for the day, was tending to her roses and doing other outdoor chores as she sat me down in the middle of the garden. She turned on the irrigation hose and went busily about her work.

As I sat there I smelled the garden's fragrances and pawed curiously at the rich soil. I felt the coolness of the slowly rising water, which soon enveloped me in a tantalizing muddiness. For the first time in my

---

28. Emanuels, *John Muir Inventor*, 24.

young life, I felt truly alive. I recall wild sensations—a kind of raw "maleness." Impulsively, I tore off my shirt and shorts, and then—naked as a jaybird—I rolled like a piglet in the muddy rivulets. My carefree soirée ended abruptly when my grandmother returned and hurriedly rushed me off to the customary scrub down. It was no little time before she finally reclaimed her grandson from the dangers of the wilderness.

The vegetable garden remained for many years until Pop put in a patio, covering over the soil with concrete. The patio was nice, but not quite like the garden. The garden promised adventure and excitement, and a little guy like me could hide among the tomato plants, becoming wild once more. Naturally, I was much too young then to understand the significance of the garden experience, but it is clear to me now. I was being schooled in the primary lesson of the wilderness. Nature was telling me, *"You are truly alive and you have a wild heart."* This is the teaching of self-awareness ... of uniqueness ... of masculinity. Learning this lesson is the first step on the road to authentic personhood.

WILD HEARTS

John Muir tells of "red-blooded playmates, wild as myself," and forbidden forays along the Dunbar coast:

> I ran away to the seashores or the fields almost every Saturday and every day in the school vacations except Sundays, though solemnly warned that I must play at home in the garden or back yard, lest I should learn to think bad thoughts and say bad words. All in vain. In spite of the sure sore punishments that followed like shadows, the natural inherited wildness in our blood ran true on its glorious course as invincible and unstoppable as stars.[29]

An outdoor experience can awaken in us a sense of being genuinely alive. It can draw out pure essences of our masculinity. As we have seen, Nature teaches her lessons in some rather unusual and unfamiliar places, and when one least expects it. For John Muir, it first began on the Scottish coast; for Bill Doulos, it was in a storm drain at the local golf course. For me, it happened in a vegetable garden and it has been happening with regularity ever since. Though a wilderness encounter may vary in the descriptors one uses, Nature seems to affect us all in very similar fashion. There is usually an element of danger, and an ever present—even tran-

29. Muir, *The Story of My Boyhood*, 1.

scendent—feeling of wildness. Is this so because at our core we truly are "wild men?" Writer John Eldredge thinks so.

In *Wild at Heart*, Eldredge provides a compelling look at the secrets of masculinity. He is fed up with nice guy images, lamenting "the westward expansion against the masculine soul," which has driven men's hearts like wounded animals into the high country. He believes that "in the heart of every man is a desperate desire for a battle to fight, an adventure to live, and a beauty to rescue."[30] While these metaphors may make some people feel a bit uneasy, the evidence is irrefutable that many men often bear deep wounds, suffered in battles fought to discover their self-identities. As John Eldridge will tell you, these wounds are often inflicted on us by our fathers. Nevertheless, a boy needs a father figure in his life. Whereas a boy's biological father may be ideally suited for this role, we do not live in an ideal world, and sometimes fathers turn up missing. Fortunately, many fine stepfathers, grandfathers, and other surrogate dads have stepped in to substitute for these absentees. As a boy grows toward maturity and seeks his identity as a man, he looks to his father for guidance and counsel. In this crucial period of the masculine lifecycle, his father becomes the essential relationship in a boy's life. This is not to diminish a mother's role, for both mother and father are equally important in a boy's development. It is only that, in the fragile metamorphosis from boy to man, the male of our species desperately needs his father.

Some men have been blessed to have spent time with their dads in the woods—hunting, fishing, hiking, and camping. I have yet to meet a man who had these experiences, who did not develop a strong bond with his father. I would not deny that many of these men were wounded by their fathers in one way or another, but the best times in a boy's life were often those spent with his hero in the great outdoors. A Nature outing was a chance for a son to see his father in a different setting. In my case, there was something refreshing—something revealing—about seeing Dad in rubber waders and a fishing vest, instead of a starched shirt and polished wingtip shoes. When he got out into Nature he seemed to open up a little, becoming more like who he probably was deep inside. More than once I saw a wildness in him; it was a good kind of wildness, and I liked it. I wanted to be wild, too, just like my father.

---

30. Eldridge, *Wild at Heart*, 9.

Such wild currents of masculinity spring forth spontaneously from the core of a boy's being, at the headwaters of his soul. Not long ago, I was reminded of just how strong a boy's deep longing to know his wild nature can be. Friends, accompanied by their grandson, Clayton, had just arrived with much anticipation at our vacation home nestled among the pine trees on the crest of the Sierras. It was Clayton's first visit to the mountains, so I was showing him around the place when suddenly he exclaimed, "I know all about the perils of the wilderness!" I immediately thought, "Good coaching, Grandpa!" I asked him what he meant by "perils," and he went on to explain that "bears live in these woods and you better watch out for rattlesnakes." I then asked him how he knew so much about the wilderness. His confident response floored me. "I knew it before I was born," he declared. Later, when I told his grandfather what Clayton had said, he was equally confounded by the boy's wisdom. "He often says things like that and I don't know where it's coming from. It makes the hair on my neck stand on end every time he says something so unexpected. I have never heard him use those words before."

Clayton lives in a rural area of New York State and since he was old enough to walk he has been drawn to the woods that surround the family's home. He loves to go fishing, feed the wild birds, and walk among the trees. He is attuned to the natural world to a degree that is unusual, especially for someone of such tender years. You see, at the time, Clayton was not yet five-years old!

Primary Lesson of the Wild

- *Self-awareness*: "I am truly alive and I have a wild heart!"

3

A Redoubtable Journey

I will lift up mine eyes unto the hills, from whence cometh my help.

—Psalm 121

WHILE GROWING UP IN Santa Cruz, California, I often succumbed to the powerful allure of the tranquil redwood groves and shaded streams that abounded in the nearby mountains. It was in these peaceful sanctuaries that I found refuge from the complexities of adolescent life. I sometimes went cave crawling, or hunted arrowheads along ancient Indian trails. In springtime, I caught frogs and tadpoles in neighboring ponds and fished for largemouth bass in the small lake at the other side of the vacant lot across the street. Out of those years I grew to become a trout fisherman, owing largely to many successful outings on secluded coastal creeks.

My father owned an insurance business in town, and I reckoned that we were pretty well off as compared to most of the families I knew. Dad had strict rules about how the household was to be run. He rigorously enforced the axiom that children should be seen and not heard, so opportunities for a father and son dialogue were infrequent. Dinner was served promptly at 5:30 p.m. each evening, and heaven help my siblings or me if we were late. Discipline was instilled into us with a stout leather belt, the force of which caused me much discomfort on numerous occasions.

My father was a good man, but he must have felt the considerable burden of his fatherly responsibilities, for he sometimes resorted to alcohol to lighten his load. It was difficult to watch him when he was drinking, and I feared the seething anger that could manifest itself during his bouts with a bottle. But then he would fight through it and remain sober for another month or two, before predictably falling off the wagon once again. With a fierce determination, Dad finally overcame his addiction, and with the help of caring friends and Alcoholics Anonymous, he remained sober for the last twenty-five years of his life.

Mom was assigned all the traditional women's chores around the house—washing, ironing, cooking, cleaning, and then some. I knew that she loved me deeply and I could confide in her about most of the things that were on my mind. My mother fostered a sense of trust and accessibility that was absent in my relationship with my father. I never quite knew where I stood with him, and this was a source of a disquieting insecurity, especially for a sensitive, impressionable boy like me. I remember many wakeful nights spent questioning and wondering—who was I and what would become of me?

I attended the local parochial school, which I walked to and from each day. Bored by most subjects, I frequently drifted off into daydreams of wild and dangerous places. Instead of taking notes in class, I sketched cascading waterfalls, leaping salmon, grizzly bears—anything that would transport me to the wilderness of my imagination. My friends wanted to grow up to be firemen or policemen or lifeguards, but I wanted to be a forest ranger.

I loved to read tales of the adventurous men of history. I longed to ride the trail with Roy Rogers and fire a breechloader like Davy Crockett. Prince Valiant was my favorite comic hero and I fantasized that I was his dashing companion, riding a white stallion and romancing a mysterious princess. My heroes were larger than life, and despite what I have revealed about him, my father was one of them. During World War II, he served in the last remaining unit of the United States Horse Cavalry. He learned to ride and rope with the best of men, and I once saw him lasso a wild deer from a moving Jeep in an open field. He broke nearly half his ribs in the process. Dad was a crack shot with a rifle, too, earning "Expert Marksman" honors in the Army. My hero could even ride a bicycle while facing backwards—downhill, no less!

My father spent as much time as he could with my brother and me. We attended the annual cattle branding and learned to shoot a rifle on the nearby Wilder Ranch, which is now a State Park. On windy days, we sometimes flew kites in the vast open fields that bordered the rugged Monterey Bay shoreline. We occasionally drove to Salinas to check on my grandfather's farm and buy vegetables from growers along country roads. I remember the time that Dad took us to the edge of town, where we cut slingshots from the forks of a generous old willow tree. We enjoyed some good times with him in those early years, and we built a bond that lasted until he died in 1998.

WILDERNESS INTRODUCTION

My first real introduction to the wilderness came suddenly and fortuitously in the spring of 1960, when I was eleven years old. Dad came home from work one evening and announced that we had been invited to spend the opening weekend of the trout-fishing season with his friends in the high Sierras. Little did I know then, but it was to be the adventure of a lifetime—three days that would change everything.

After a few fits and starts, we finally arrived late on Friday evening at the rustic little cabin on the fringes of Yosemite National Park. We rolled out our sleeping bags onto metal cots and ceremoniously arranged our fishing gear in anticipation of the following day's activities. We met other men there, but none quite like the venerable old character named "Doc," who tantalized us with extraordinary accounts of his wild times in the mountains. Married to an Indian woman, Doc had trekked for thousands of miles on alpine trails, filled bathtubs to overflowing with a days catch, and at the age of seventy, been treed for several hours by an angry bear. It mattered not that he embellished his tales, Doc was a powerful storyteller and he had us—hook, line and sinker!

Early on Saturday morning, we set out to fish the Tuolumne River and then several spring creeks with forgotten names. I was mesmerized as I watched Dad's friend, Jerry, rhythmically cast a dry-fly to anxious trout in a winding meadow stream. Every precious daylight moment was consumed with hiking and fishing and living. I cannot now remember how many fish I caught that day; my creel could have been empty, but my soul was brimming. In the evening we went to the adjacent garbage dump where we waited anxiously, then watched as several black bears foraged hopefully among the tin cans and cardboard boxes. Shrouded in darkness, we marveled at the many shooting stars that streaked brilliantly across the sky. Finally, exhausted and joyful, I fell asleep and dreamed the dreams that only an experience in the wilderness can bring. It had been the best day of my life.

Each spring or summer for some years thereafter, we returned to that sacred place along the Evergreen Road to the Hetch Hetchy reservoir. While each renewal was life-giving, there never was a time like the first. Reflecting back, it would be difficult to overestimate the importance of that moment in my history. It was my first initiation into manhood and I will be forever grateful to the men who made it all possible.

Benchmark outdoor experiences like mine just ooze with meaning. It was during this time that I began to acquire a deep regard for the world of Nature, and I envisioned that one day I might earn my place in the company of men. It was clearly the time of life when Nature began to instill in me one of her vital lessons. It is the lesson of humility, and it is indubitable: *"I am part of something much bigger."* (Remember Richard Rohr's truths of male initiation: You are not that important! You are not in control!). Nature has shown me time and again that there is a grand story being orchestrated in the symphony that is life, and that each one of us has a small but important part to play in it. Each time I am in her world, I am humbled by Nature's simplicity and by her complexity; by her strength and her splendor. Countless times, I have been blessed by the integrity of the wilderness.

CHIMERAS

Someone who knew him well once told me that my father was jealous of me for the success I had achieved during my professional career and family life. In time, I came to understand that his "jealousy" had nothing to do with me; in fact, it was not jealousy at all. While Dad was successful by most measures, in some ways he lived a life of unfulfilled promise. He was battling the chimeras of false expectations—expectations thrust on him by others, particularly his parents.

I was his eldest son and perhaps in me he saw his own youthful reflection, filled with wonder and anticipation. I was the first member of my immediate family to receive a college degree, to move more than a few miles from home, and to seek a new and independent life in places of my own choosing. I had relocated to southern California, where I met and married a woman who was not entirely acceptable to my father. I found a new church and made new friendships. I began to achieve a modest level of financial independence, and as the years passed, I became more and more self-reliant. These departures were bitter pills for Dad to swallow.

My father was not unlike many men I have met who are burdened with the knowledge that the road ahead is getting shorter; the great promise of youth may not be fully realized. Many men live with deep regrets about their lives: they didn't go back to school, start their own business, marry someone else, have children. The list is endless, and a man can become beset by vain imaginings of how things might have been better if only he had followed a different course. The dawn of life turns all too quickly into noonday, and the sun presses on toward twilight—time is running short! I became painfully aware of the limitations of time when something entirely unforeseen happened to me in 1996.

I had been employed with the Procter & Gamble Company since my discharge from the Army—for nearly twenty-four years. I was now in my middle forties, with a wife and two children, facing significant personal and financial obligations. On a fateful October morning, I was given notice that my job was being eliminated. For the first time in my life, I felt unwanted and insignificant. Numbed with fear, I took the downward trail into darkness.

After the initial shock and period of denial and disbelief, I entered the abyss of anger and resentment. A man can lose his way in such cold and forbidding places. I was on a lonely journey, but through counseling and the encouragement of family and friends, I slowly began to claw my way back from the depths. Though I had scarcely picked up a book since my college days, I began reading voraciously. In the year following my job loss, I read more than a hundred books, cover to cover—philosophy, science, nature, history, theology—anything dealing with truth and significance. I enrolled at a leading theological seminary, where I studied leadership and the lives of great women and men. I spent an increasing amount of time in contemplation and reflection; and, once again, I turned to Nature to help me redefine my life's purpose and rediscover the vitality that once had energized and given meaning to my life.

As I had so often done in my youth, I sought the solitude of the mountains—hiking and fishing, wondering and questioning. On occasion I would make the three-hour drive from Los Angeles to the upper reaches of the Kern River, where I would spend the day fly-fishing. I have fished some of the finest rivers and streams in North America, but the Kern tops my list. For miles on end, cold crystal-clear water pours over stones of endless shape and color—shades of red and yellow and green. The flatter sections of the river are made up of broad emerald pools, some as much as eighty feet across. But in the narrows of the canyons, the current rips across polished granite with incredible ferocity, belying the impression of peace and calm that one senses from the shoreline. In springtime, the Kern can be treacherous, but by mid-summer she is transformed into a dry-fly fisherman's paradise. The Kern is a dangerous place, but it is also a place where a man can recover his soul.

The river is populated by squawfish, the only game fish native to the upper Kern. These denizens of the deep, while they are not good eating and are seldom caught, reach three feet in length and can weigh over twenty pounds. Just to see fish of these proportions is an experience in itself. The river is also home to an exceptional strain of rainbow trout, which reach considerable size as well. These trout are highly aggressive, sometimes moving several feet to attack a fly. These were the attractions that led me to the Kern on one memorable occasion in June of 1997.

I left home before dawn and drove to Kernville, the stepping-off point for rafters, hikers, and fishermen. After a hot breakfast in the little café in town, I drove the remaining twenty miles along the Kern until I reached the parking lot at the Johnsondale Bridge. It was mid-week and there were only a couple of cars in the lot, signaling that I would have little company along the river. Perfect!

After hiking along the river trail for an hour or so, I assembled my rod, tied on my favorite fly, and waded out into the current. As it usually does, it took me a few minutes to get my casting rhythm going, but before long I was right in sync. Then, suddenly, and without warning, I was overcome with emotion. I found myself repeating these three words: "You're still here! You're still here!" I had been slowly, unknowingly absorbed into the beauty around me. Everything seemed to downshift into low gear; I was in ultra-slow motion. It was as if a peace was flowing into me and I was becoming part of the river itself. Though I was present in time and space, I felt as if I had somehow gone beyond it. I do not know how else to describe what happened, except to say that I have never experienced anything in my life that was so deeply moving.

I have since discovered that there are many other men who have been overtaken by this same feeling of timeless unity; of perfect comradeship; of being loved. Gerald May describes what he calls "the Presence" that he frequently encountered in Nature:

> I don't know where or how the gift of grace might come. In those outdoor-wilderness years I called it the Power of the Slowing, the incarnate mercy of Absolute Nature moving into willingness, opening my desire, deepening my relaxation, empowering my vulnerability, making me receptive to what is. It happens very rarely now, but Wisdom does still come to me that way sometimes, as if Her hands were touching my belly and massaging my shoulders and turning my head so I can really see and feel what is here and know who I truly am.[1]

As he wrote these words, May knew that he was losing his battle with cancer. But somehow his outdoor experiences had given him the wisdom to recognize that he too was a player on a bigger stage; that dying was just part of the *paradox of hidden wholeness*. Gerald May departed in 2005.

In a most remarkable way, May's story intersects with my own. I, too, have felt the immeasurable "Power of the Slowing," and, after many reunions, have become well acquainted with the Presence. I have grown accustomed to listening for voices that can be heard in the wild. I did not always hear these voices, and it should come as no surprise that it was a duckbuilder who first taught me how to listen.

VOICES IN THE WILD

"Do you hear it?" Jim whispered. "Hear what?" I asked, as I tilted my head to listen for some elusive noise. Jim was my father-in-law and we were fishing an uncrowded section of the Truckee River near Reno, Nevada. He was a gentle man; an accomplished painter, dancer, musician, and fisherman. Jim could cast a spinner with an artistry that I have seen neither before nor since. He could also bait you with a subtle humor that was all his own. "Can't you hear it?" he persisted. I stood motionless for a minute or two, but detected nothing. Jim smiled at me, then quietly turned away and headed downstream, leaving me wondering whether my frustration was over being cajoled, or because he was catching most of the trout that morning. For the rest of the afternoon I fished solo and pondered my en-

---

1. May, *The Wisdom of Wilderness*, 83.

counter with this wise old fisherman. He was in his sixties and had spent a lifetime in the woods, hunting and fishing. Perhaps there was something that he was trying to teach me. What was I missing?

I never again had to ask Jim what sounds he heard along the Truckee River that day, for I soon heard them for myself. I have since heard them again and again. These sounds are not audible, at least not in the way we commonly understand sound to be. They are muted, yet discernible, persistent, and reassuring.

I get a spine tingling sensation when I hear Robert Redford's mystic words in the concluding scene of the film, *A River Runs Through It*.

> Eventually all things merge into one, and a river runs through it. The river was cut by the world's great flood and runs over rocks from the basement of time. On some of the rocks are timeless raindrops. Under the rocks are the words, and some of the words are theirs. *I am haunted by waters.*[2]

Though we fished the same stretch of water, Jim and I each experienced the river in perfect solitude. I am sure that he must have heard those still, gentle voices many times before. There was for me no sound, no calling voices, until the sacred silence opened me up—when I had the willingness to receive the gift of grace. Now, the sounds of silence are ever present in the wild, calling out to me. I, too, am a man who is haunted by waters. I am haunted, also, by a duckbuilder's beckoning call from just around the river's bend: "You are not alone." No, I am not alone! This is the lesson of faith, the faith that there will be another wilderness just over the horizon—a wilderness surpassing even our wildest dreams.

Meditating on the glories of what he called "the singing wilderness," a great woodsman once noted:

> I have discovered that I am not alone in my listening; that almost everyone is listening for something—that the search for places where the singing may be heard goes on everywhere. It seems to be part of the hunger that all of us have for a time when we were closer to lakes and rivers, to mountains and meadows and forests, than we are today.[3]

---

2. Maclean, *A River Runs Through It*, 104.
3. Olson, *The Singing Wilderness*, 6.

THE WISDOM OF FLY-FISHING

I now live in southern California, where we are blessed with ready access to the natural world. We have hundreds of miles of scenic hiking trails, numerous mountain peaks to climb, and world-class parks and gardens. Unfortunately, these settings are often overcrowded and noisy, so that one never truly experiences the full force of the wild. Whether hiking or fishing, I have had my best days in more remote locations where it is quiet and less populated. Nowadays, most of my outdoor travels take me to places that I can experience with a fly-rod in my hand.

Over the years, I have met many people who are novices in their understanding of the art of fly-fishing. I chuckled the first time someone told me that it was inhumane to run a hook through an innocent fly. I have been asked more than once how it is possible for the weight of a fly to propel such a heavy line. Actually, living creatures are never used to bait a fly fisherman's hook. Flies are made of natural and synthetic materials that are tied to a hook in order to simulate insects, or other entrées on a fish's menu. It is the weight of the line and the flexing power of the rod that enable an angler to cast a fly.

No one knows with certainty where or when fly-fishing originated. Archaeologists have unearthed fish hooks that are at least thirty thousand years old, so it may be impossible to determine when an innovative fisherman first tied on a few feathers to make an artificial fly. We are fairly certain that the Macedonians of the first or second century used wax to apply wool and feathers to a hook, to attract "fish with speckled skin" on the River Astraeus.[4] Regardless of its precise origins, fly-fishing has enjoyed a continuous popularity for hundreds of years.

Becoming an accomplished fly fisherman can take a long time. While casting can be learned with a few lessons and a couple of outings, the subtleties of "reading the water" and "managing drag" in heavy currents is learned the old fashioned way—through trial and error. The dry-fly fisherman's task is to appeal to the trout's appetite by replicating a living insect bobbing along on the surface of the water. This deception requires that the imitation must drift naturally in the currents, just like the real thing. Getting the fly to the right spot for a good drift, so as not to spook the fish, requires proper technique and a special coordination. There is a

---

4. Herd, "A Flyfishing History," para. 4.

poetic motion in casting with a fly rod that seems to draw a man into a rhythm with the world around him.

At the other end of the fly line is the trout. Trout surely occupy a special place in the realm of the Infinite. Since water first flowed on Earth, these silvery beings must have lurked among the rocks and riffles, looking for their next meal. While they mostly feed below the surface of the water, the presence of a floating bug can transform a hungry trout into a violent splash of pure intentionality. There is an indescribable rush of adrenalin when everything comes together and the trout rises to take the fly. In my youth, I was often too tense during the play of the fish to fully appreciate the moment. Now, having caught more than my fair share of them, the actual landing of the trout is not as important as the bond that unites us at the moment he is hooked. For me, above all else, fly-fishing has become a form of communication. When a trout is on my line, I feel vibrant and alive. I have a deep synergistic connection to the natural world. I am "plugged in" to something beyond the visible—something of which I am already a part . . . and something of which I yearn to know more about. When linked to a trout, I sense the sublime inter-relationship of created things. And I am aware that there is more—much more.

An important feature of fly-fishing is the conservation ethic that it promotes. The majority of fly fisherman practice "catch-and-release," where the fish is carefully netted and then returned unharmed back into the water. Fly fishermen recognize that trout are a renewable resource, and that the only way to insure the future of the sport is to preserve trout habitat. Hundreds of miles of our finest rivers have been set aside exclusively for catch-and-release fishing, where only single, barbless hooks are permitted. Owing to the efforts of organizations like Trout Unlimited, Caltrout, and local casting clubs, native trout populations have been reintroduced into many lakes and streams. Marine biologists and state Department of Fish and Game officials work closely with clubs, fly shops, and concerned citizens to insure that the next generation of fly fishermen will be able to connect with a wild trout.

Fishing can play a pivotal role in a child's development. If a boy fishes frequently enough with his dad or other mentor, he is more likely to become a fisherman himself and someday teach his own children how to fish. As my own experience suggests, a boy can gain powerful insights into manhood by observing men in a natural setting. There is no better way for a father to spend time with his son or daughter than to take them fishing.

Tom Shenk is a talented business consultant with a highly successful leadership development practice. While he spends much of his time in company board rooms, Tom's true passion lies in the middle of a trout steam. He became an accomplished fly fisherman due to the influence of his father, who taught him a deep abiding love for the outdoors. Tom will now tell you that the best moments in his life are those when he is fly-fishing, especially when accompanied by his sons, John and Bob. When "Johnny" was eight-years old, Tom took him on a fishing trip to the Big Wood River in Idaho. He hoped that their experience on this blue ribbon trout water would begin to instill in his son a passion for the adventure of fly-fishing. More importantly, Tom wanted to teach Johnny the power of Nature in forging the bond between a father and a son. As it turned out, their time together became a watershed event for both men.

In every detail, Tom meticulously retells their story: "So I am on the Big Wood and I am with my eight year old son. It is his first fly-fishing experience with me. It is fairly wide, although in most cases a good cast can get across the river. I get to a bend in the river where I can teach my son how to cast. There is a natural flow of the drift. There is a wind . . ." After giving Johnny some initial instruction, Tom heads downstream and begins fishing himself. He glances frequently upriver, proudly watching as his son gains confidence as a fly fisherman. After landing several small fish, Tom notices a feeding trout, prodigiously slurping down bugs on the surface of the water at the far side of the river. This is no ordinary fish, and Tom promptly names him "Big Lips." Big Lips did not grow to trophy size by being foolish; his home is situated beneath the cover of some overhanging branches, where it would take a flawless delivery to correctly present a dry-fly. As his son watches, Tom attempts numerous casts, but the evening breezes and the swirling currents do not allow for a good drift. Even his best efforts result in a float of only a few inches before the fly is swept away. After about fifteen minutes of frustrated attempts to lure Big Lips from his lair, Tom tells Johnny, "The sun is going down, Mom is cooking dinner. Well I think that's it. I can't get that fish." Johnny, who is not yet ready to call it a day, implores: "Dad, oh no! Let's not quit. Give it one more try." Tom remembers: "Suddenly, the wind drops. Everything is perfect. I look back and my kid has this beautiful angelic look on his face. And I make this cast . . ." Then something miraculous happens. The fly hits the overhanging branches and drops gently into the water. Tom gets about a foot-and-a-half of drift . . . whack! Big Lips is hooked, and so is Johnny. After a valiant fight, the big trout is brought to the bank, admired, and then gently slipped back into the coldness of the river. Neither of these men will ever forget their magic moment together on the Big Wood.

Over the years, Tom spent an equal amount of time with his son, Bob, who is no less an outdoorsman than his older brother. So successful was he in introducing his sons to the world of Nature that Bob has formally asked Tom to take the lead in his own son's outdoor education. Tom is honored by this request and is bubbling with anticipation at the prospects of exploring the wilderness with his grandson at his side.

A River Runs Through It is Norman Maclean's mythic story of a pastor's family living near the banks of the Big Blackfoot River in western Montana during the early decades of the 1900s. The principal characters are two brothers, who are struggling to make the arduous passage into manhood. Though they are as different as a caddis fly and a June bug, they discover that fly fishing is the spiritual bond that unites them. The story begins:

> In our family, there was no clear line between religion and fly-fishing. We lived at the junction of great trout waters in western Montana and our father was a Presbyterian minister and a fly fisherman who tied his own flies and taught others. He told us about Christ's disciples being fishermen and we were left to assume, as my brother and I did, that all first-class fishermen on the Sea of Galilee were fly fishermen and that John, the favorite, was a dry-fly fisherman.[5]

Norman, the eldest of the brothers, is very much like his father—conservative, focused, and caring. Paul, on the other hand, dances to an entirely different beat. Though he is brash, self-centered, and compulsive, he is also immensely gifted as a fly fisherman. There is a wildfire raging inside him, which burns uncontrollably until it is extinguished when Paul is beaten to death for failing to pay his gambling debts. In summing up his brother's life, Norman tells his father, "All I really know is that he was a fine fisherman." His father replies, "You know more than that . . . he was beautiful!" Norman responds, "Yes, he was beautiful. He should have been—you taught him."[6] This was the last time that the two men spoke of Paul's death.

5. Maclean, *A River Runs Through It*, 1.
6. Ibid., 103.

Nature's lessons are more easily taught in the company of a competent guide and good companions. When the guide is a boy's father, another dimension is added to the experience of learning. Although Paul's brilliance flashed for but an instant in the streams of time, he was of a wildness that few of us will ever know. He had learned his outdoor lessons well. Paul *was* beautiful . . . and he was truly alive!

Fly-fishing is a spiritual pursuit. If a man fishes long enough, sooner or later he will come to the realization, like Thoreau, that it is not fish he is after.

Lessons of the Wild

- *Self-awareness:* "I am truly alive and I have a wild heart!"
- *Humility:* "I am part of something much bigger."
- *Faith:* "I am not alone."

4

Teacher Rattlesnake

Unless all of creation is a revelation, no particular revelation is possible.

—William Temple

THE SIGHT OF A rattlesnake is something that I can do without. However, many of my favorite outdoor destinations are hotbeds for these scary reptiles, and in my travels I have seen more than I can remember; so many, in fact, that I fully expect to see one each time I take to the trail. I use extreme caution when I am in snake country, but once in a while I inadvertently aggravate a rattler and on two occasions I narrowly escaped their deadly bite. Unfortunately, when it comes to rattlesnakes, I seem to have a magnetic personality.

A few years ago, as I prepared to hike up a lonely mountain trail, I had a powerful premonition that I was about to have yet another rattlesnake encounter. As it turned out, my instincts were terrifyingly correct. In making my way up the trail, I was keeping a sharp lookout for spots where a rattlesnake would likely be concealed, when suddenly a three-footer came cascading down the sloping hillside and settled right at my feet. Startled, I stumbled backwards and hopped onto a large boulder. Unlike many of the rattlers that I have come across, this determined Diamondback seemed completely oblivious to my presence. Instead, he was clearly focused on finding his lunch among the rocks and shrubs bordering the trail. The snake went stealthily about his business, while I tried to relax and get my blood pressure to subside. Rather than make my usual hasty retreat, I decided that this time I would take a few minutes to observe the snake's movements.

The rattlesnake is a cleverly designed creature that glides effortlessly along with a mesmerizing grace. Though it has limited eyesight, the rattler has a laser tongue that operates like a heat seeking probe, detecting minute changes in the surrounding temperatures and enabling it to isolate its prey with stunning precision. Rattlesnakes are acutely sensitive to vibration and can immediately gauge if an intruder is a prospective meal, or a threat. The mottled markings on their skin can vary in color, providing an ideal camouflage in almost any terrain. Rattlesnakes are part of Nature's elegant balance of scarcity and abundance. When populations of its prey are high, the snakes thrive; when populations decline, so do the number of rattlers. I thought about all these things as I watched the snake slither smoothly ahead. Then, it went off the trail, where it instantly disappeared among the dry oak leaves.

I had never noticed before how dangerously beautiful rattlesnakes are. Perhaps the whims of evolution account for their presence and perfect adaptation to their lowland world; or, as many people believe, the rattlesnake could only have originated in the creative mind of an intelligent designer. I know a few people who so revile them that they would readily accept the notion that the rattler was planted here as a cruel experiment by scientists from an alien world. Given this reptile's remarkable characteristics, I suppose that any one of these explanations is possible. But I am inclined to believe that the snake's presence here on Earth may mark a deeper significance.

Judeo-Christian mythology tells of Satan's fall from power and of his banishment by God to an infinitely dark underworld. Satan, while he can take a pleasing shape, is often depicted as a serpent. He employed this disguise when he fooled Adam and Eve into eating the forbidden fruit of the Tree of Knowledge in the Garden of Eden. Snakes have had a bad rap since word of this beguilement leaked out. The common misconception of myths like this one is that they are only fantasy, that mythology never embodies truth. But myth is a way of telling a story that would otherwise be beyond the limits of human comprehension. Myths can actually represent real people, places, and historical events. Myths can be true.

So, where do snakes fit in? For, while they are creatures of myth and legend, they are also quite real. I am convinced that snakes are here to remind us of the extraordinariness of life. The element of danger present in a close encounter with a venomous snake awakens our primal fears, hyper-stimulates the senses, and provides an incredible rush of adrenalin. The hearts pounds, the skin flushes, and the circuits of the brain strain to take in data. Where is the snake? How far away? How big is it? All the while there is this indescribable feeling of being truly alive—of being connected in a very elemental way to the seemingly limitless world of living beings. The rattlesnake is a paradoxical creature. It reminds us that there is a dark side to our world of light. It teaches us that we can be courageous, even as we are paralyzed by fear; that we can learn something about love from a creature that evokes feelings of hatred. Perhaps it is only when we have seen the face of death in the form of a serpent that we begin to appreciate the deep meaning of life.

Seeing that rattlesnake on the trail has helped me to know that darkness and fear and hate and death are simply part of the *paradox of hidden wholeness* underlying all of Creation. Nature engenders tolerance, continuously offering novel ways for wayfarers on the wilderness trail to comprehend the amazing complexities of our world. *All of life is beautiful!*

ANIMAL MESSENGERS

Wild animals like the rattlesnake have appeared in my path with a regularity that seems to defy coincidence. For Native Americans, however, the appearance of an animal is no mere happenstance. Indians have long known that Nature's movements are rife with meaning, and that animals are often harbingers of things to come. In Indian mythology, members of the animal kingdom are assigned human—and sometimes superhuman—characteristics as creators, messengers, and guides. Coyote, the *trickster*, takes on human form and is associated alternatively with creation and with death. In the Hopi tradition, a great water snake is responsible for the springs that flow from the ground. The buffalo, the universal Indian symbol of generosity and fertility, once provided the Indian with all of his basic needs. Indian healers, called *shamans*, are thought to have animal guides as they pass through the supernatural world, and birds are afterlife guides for the spirits of the dead.

During the past several years, I have become increasingly sensitive to what appear to be Nature's clues to a reality beyond the plainly visible.

I recall the moment when I first began to see that animals might actually play an indispensable role in revealing this reality.

My wilderness companion and I had awakened early from a restless first night's sleep on the trail. As we stood glassy-eyed around the campfire waiting for the coffee to perk, two shadowy movements in the tree line just above our camp caught our attention. We watched as a pair of mule deer emerged cautiously from the woods and cocked their heads in our direction. As one of them picked up our scent and quickly bounded off, the other sauntered straight towards us. We stood perfectly still as the curious doe entered our campsite. Apparently, she had met campers before, for she fearlessly began sniffing her way through our gear. Satisfied that there was nothing she could eat, she directed her attention toward the two humans standing attentively nearby. She approached to within a single step of me, and for a brief instant we made eye contact. With her gaze, the deer seemed to say in her humble sort of way that she was giving us a treasure—the simple gift of her presence. In that moment, I saw a part of life that is pure and innocent. I felt a certain warmth—almost a kind of hospitality—and I knew something of the deep kinship we humans have with wild animals. This encounter proved to me that if we are in tune with the Creation, there is a possibility of communicating directly with other living beings. A willing heart opens us to receive the blessings of Nature's abundance. The wild deer was an emissary on a visitation of peace and she acknowledged us as fellow travelers through the wild. She was beautiful. She was pure giftedness.

BEARS

Few sights in Nature evoke more awe and respect than that of a fully-grown bear. With regard to humans, North American black bears have two orientations: wild bears and those known as "camp bears." Camp bears have lost most of their instinctive fears and they have acquired some bad manners when it comes to Nature's two-legged visitors. Because these bears are such masterful thieves, steel boxes have had to be installed in many recreation areas to protect campers' food supplies. For as little temptation as a bag of chips or a candy bar, bears have been known to open up an automobile like it was a sardine tin. If you have never seen the carnage at a campsite after a hungry bruin has raided it, I can tell you, it is something to behold!

Wild bears are found in the backcountry, far away from busy tourist destinations. They have retained most of their primitive instincts and are far less visible than camp bears. Wild bears are still curious enough to visit a campsite though, which they typically do under the cover of darkness. Many a wilderness camper has had a horrifying experience with these burly nighttime intruders. Although black bears have approached to within a few feet of me, I have never been afraid of them. But in the wilds of Alaska, I have been absolutely terrified that I might cross paths with a grizzly bear. Gerald May offers a revealing expression of the fear that a man can feel during a bear encounter. May writes:

> For the first time in my life, I am experiencing pure fear. I am completely present in it, in a place beyond all coping because there is nothing to do. I have never before experienced such clean, unadulterated purity of emotion. This fear is naked. It consists, in these slowly passing moments, of my heart pounding, my breath rushing yet fully silent, my body ready for anything, my mind absolutely empty, open, waiting. I am fear. It is beautiful.[1]

Such transparent expressions of raw emotion—particularly for men—are rare. It is noteworthy that the wilderness was the setting and that a bear was the messenger. It is unlikely that learning moments like this one could have happened amidst the busyness of the city, where the only bears are caged in the local zoo.

Late in his journey, in one final quest to understand the meaning of his life, Gerald May embarked on a series of solitary wilderness adventures. He had never spent much time in the woods and was unprepared for what awaited him, but he gambled that Nature held clues to the riddle of existence. May's gamble paid off. His final book, *The Wisdom of Wilderness*, is not only a gem of storytelling genius, but is a passionate account of one man's courageous attempt to find congruence between his inner wilderness and the wilds of the natural world.

SACRED PLACES

Most of us who have seen bears know only their public side, but they have a private side, too. Bears take a few months off during the winter to rest from the ardors of wilderness survival. Year after year they return

---

1. May, *The Wisdom of Wilderness*, 32.

to hibernate in the same den that they may have used for generations. Sows give birth to their cubs in the privacy of these dens, which are well concealed in the remotest of places. The chances of discovering a bear's den are very slim and would be considered an exceptional find by anyone. Frank and John Craighead, who pioneered grizzly bear research in Yellowstone National Park from 1959 until the 1970s, were so lucky.

The Craighead's were seasoned outdoorsmen, who proved that it was possible for man and the grizzly bear to peaceably coexist. As a young man, I can recall watching a National Geographic television special featuring the Craighead brothers camping in Yellowstone and studying the bears. One could not help but be inspired by their passion and their commitment to the preservation of life.

Today, due largely to their efforts, the grizzly bear is no longer considered a threat to human survival and can still be seen in some regions of the Park. Frank Craighead writes, "These magnificent creatures are in many ways the epitome of evolutionary adaptation, but in order to survive in today's world, they need our understanding. Without it they are doomed."[2] Without the bear and without his wild spirit, our own species is doomed, as well. Frank and John Craighead are among a select group of people who have been formally recognized by the National Geographic Society for distinguished contributions to humanity through wildlife conservation. In being so honored, they took their place alongside other duckbuilders like Jacques Cousteau, Sir Edmund Hillary, Richard and Mary Leakey, and Jane Goodall.[3]

I once had the privilege of finding a bear's den in a faraway and dangerous place. At the time of the discovery, my fishing partner and I were literally "between a rock and a hard place." On the advice of an old friend who had been to the area some forty years before, we were in search of the "Holy Grail" of trout streams. My friend estimated that he caught nearly a hundred trout in one day's fishing there; he also saw more than a dozen rattlesnakes along the waters edge. With my natural affinity for rattlers, I could not have been more conflicted as we left our campsite late that morning.

There was no trail to follow, so we were inching along with a map and a compass, combined with a little "dead reckoning." We had hiked for about three hours when we finally arrived at a pristine stream, which

---

2. Craighead, preface to *Track of the Grizzly*.
3.. Martin, "Frank Craighead, 85," para. 17.

looked like it had not been fished for several seasons, perhaps even longer. After an hour of trying our luck, our enthusiasm ebbed, for we realized that there was not a single trout in the stream. With only a few hours of daylight remaining, we elected to return to camp by what we thought would be a shorter, more direct route. After following the stream for about a mile, we came to a twisted tangle of mountain shrubbery that seemed all but impassable. But the map confirmed that we were headed in the direction of the main trail, so we doggedly bushwhacked our way ahead. As we went, we could not help but notice that there were bear signs everywhere. Then, we abruptly came to the end of the trail—a precipice that fell straight down for at least three hundred feet. Either we had to head back the way we came, or negotiate a crumbly shale cliff to escape. As we surveyed our options, we spied a dark recess at the base of the cliff, which was almost completely hidden behind a dense growth of Manzanita bushes. Upon closer investigation, we confirmed by the abundance of hair and other markings that it was a bear's den. It was already late in the afternoon, so we lingered only briefly at the bruin's hideaway before climbing up the cliff. By some miracle, we were able to find the main trail and get safely back to camp before nightfall.

That night I did not sleep much, as I pondered my intrusion into the secret world of bears. I fancied that, much like Goldilocks in the storybook, I had been an uninvited guest with a remarkable tale to tell. A bear's den is a sacred and humble place: it represents the continuing birth and rebirth that is creation. This experience was a reminder that the renewal of life is as "perennial as the grass," that there will come yet another chance to start anew. Those of us who live in the world of people can easily get bogged down in the vicissitudes of everyday living and miss opportunities for new beginnings. Yes, life is hard. But every moment and every situation presents us with choices and a second chance. After all, what man is not blessed with new possibilities as he revels in the glory of a desert sunrise? Who among us does not feel a sense of great expectation as she touches the freshness of the glistening dew on an April's morn?

I am certain that my discovery of the bear's den was no coincidence. It is likely that bears have used this place for hundreds of years, yet it took me but one visit there to learn another of Nature's vital lessons. It is the lesson of hope. In the wilderness: *Life is abundant with new opportunities.*

CONNECTEDNESS OF LIFE

Have you ever wondered why humans are the only beings on Earth who wear clothing, or why it is that we bother with toilet tissue, hairbrushes, and perfume, while other creatures do not? These may not seem like the weightiest questions you will ever face, but behind their simple façade we find answers that derive from deep fundamental truths.

We are hopelessly bound to all living things, and yet we are irrefutably different from any other creature that we know of. Anthropologists tell us that the human blueprint, called DNA, is nearly identical with that of other primates. The chimpanzee, considered to be our nearest relative in the animal kingdom, has a gene set that is purportedly about ninety-nine percent the same as ours.[4] If chimpanzees—who do indeed look very much like us—are so nearly human, then why don't they write a book or design an automobile? Mechanical answers about relative brainpower and different evolutionary channels seem insufficient to explain the astonishing differences between us humans and our animal cousins. While these differences are the subject of much scientific study and intellectual scrutiny, our similarities offer the most obvious signs of our sense of earthly belonging.

Do you not find it serendipitous that our species has so many of the characteristics of other creatures? Our hands and fingers are like those of a monkey. We use the same organs and sensory mechanisms as other mammals do to hear, see, smell, taste, and touch our world. We have body hair, give off odors, and reproduce in much the same fashion as other animals do. We live; we die—no different from all other earthly inhabitants. With certitude, evolutionists cite our commonalities with animals as primary evidence for our development from other life forms. Though no one has yet discovered the precise chain of descent from animals to humans, many scientists remain optimistic that we will one day be able to trace our ancestry back to the primordial swamp where sentient life first emerged.

Creationists are skeptical about the Theory of Evolution, choosing to believe instead that life was formed as an act of love by the hand of God. "The inception of life is too mysterious to be understood," says the creationist. So he simply accepts it on faith. The Creator endowed us humans with traits similar to members of the animal kingdom, insuring that

---

4. There are numerous sources to support the strong correlation between human and chimpanzee DNA. See Ritter, "Scientists Unravel Chimpanzee DNA Sequence," para. 9. See also, Wilson, *Biophilia*, 130.

we would possess a sense of connectedness to the great web of life. After all, why would an intelligent designer produce a species that was utterly different from all others? However one views our origins, it seems abundantly clear that human beings have a rightful place in the living order of planet Earth.

MAN'S DILEMMA

Despite the knowledge that he holds a high rank among earthly species, man is faced with a nagging ontological dilemma. How can he be a creature of flesh and bone, while at the same time possessing tangible clues to unseen realities? Our fundamental differences from other animals are differences, not in *degree*, but differences of *kind*. The ape "knows," but man "knows that he knows"; it is this self-consciousness that distinguishes humans from all other creatures. *Homo sapiens* is singular in his capacity for self-transcendence—to be able to stand outside of himself and make judgments about the past, the present, and the future. As has been noted, "Man is the only animal who laughs or cries, because he is the only animal who knows the difference between the way things are and the way things ought to be."[5] No other being on Earth has demonstrated an awareness of his eventual demise, thus humans are singly possessed of the dread of death. Reinhold Neibuhr capably sums up our dilemma when he says, "Man has always been his own most vexing problem."[6]

This vexing problem became the life's work of Ernest Becker (1925–75). Becker is best known for his Pulitzer Prize winning book, *The Denial of Death*, a critical analysis of man's internal conflicts and his attempts to reconcile them. He concludes that our innate fear of death is the mainspring for all our activities, and that we attempt to transcend this mortal fear in "culturally standardized ways through heroism, narcissism, charisma, religion, and even neurosis."[7] In a brutally candid observation, he refers to humans as, ". . . a god who shits." Ultimately, if we are hon-

---

5. Quote is generally attributed to William Hazlitt, nineteenth century British essayist.

6. Neibuhr, *The Nature and Destiny of Man*, 1. Neibuhr (1892–1971), social theorist and existentialist, was a leading figure of the Christian *neo-orthodoxy* movement of the first half of the twentieth century; prominent figures included such theologians as Karl Barth, Dietrich Bonhoeffer, and Paul Tillich.

7. Becker, from the summary on the jacket of *The Denial of Death*. Becker pioneered multi-disciplinary research linking science, the humanities, social action, and religion.

est with ourselves, we are forced to accept the stark reality of our final destiny on Earth. Someday we will die; as Becker says, "going the way of the grasshopper."

In the wilderness, we are plainly confronted by the specter of death. Nowhere else is death portrayed so transparently . . . so forcefully . . . so abundantly. Nature makes no attempt to conceal death; it is everywhere. There is a great irony in seeing a trout squirming futilely in the talons of a soaring osprey, or in discovering the mangled carcass of a trophy mule deer brought down by the brute force of a mountain lion. Nature is teeming with life, but she also reminds us that there will be an end. Like the once popular bumper sticker prophesied: "Life's a bitch, then you die!" Again, we are reminded of one of Richard Rohr's key truths of male initiation: death is the natural consequence of living. The osprey and the mountain lion cannot survive without the trout and the deer; we humans will not long endure without the osprey and the mountain lion. Some must perish in order that others may live. We are all brothers on the pilgrimage to wholeness.

It is simple enough to put these words down on a page, but the notion of one's mortality is a difficult fate to have to cope with. Perhaps, as life goes on and it becomes increasingly evident that the road we are on is winding down, men and women are more inclined to think of death. But many of us have deep fears about our earthly end and we choose to flatly ignore the flashing yellow warning lights up ahead. We simply hit the "activity accelerator," insuring that will not have time to dwell on such things as the morbidity of death. In our efforts to make sense of it all, many of us find solace in the religious view that life has a meaning, that our existence has a purpose, that there is something more. Strict empiricism, on the other hand, holds that there is nothing beyond the observable—nothing other than what we can experience. "What you see is what you get!" Theologians, atheists, and other thinkers from the widest spectrum of philosophical inquiry have long debated the question of life's purpose (or purposelessness). But, in Nature's world there is no room for such debate. All living organisms—every plant, every animal, every human being—exist for one another in a sublime harmony that should elicit wonder from even the most ardent of skeptics. In the wilderness a man learns that he is fully alive, that he is part of a grand symphony, that he is never alone, and that there are endless opportunities for new beginnings. He is also confronted by the most sobering reality of all; it is the lesson of unadulterated honesty. In Nature's world, a man knows: *I am going to die!*

It seems contradictory that Nature can be teeming with life and endless opportunities for new beginnings, yet so earnestly schooling us in the ways of death. But Nature is not a contradictory place; everything exists in balance in her world. Nature is the place of paradox, where things that at first seem to defy rational explanation, upon closer investigation, reveal the mysterious tension of opposites: darkness and light, fear and courage, despair and hope. In Nature, death begets life. This is the revelation of the wild.

THE ILLUSION OF THE CITY

The place where most of us now live—the city—is no place to apprehend the paradoxical relationship between life and death. Although corporal death abounds there, our cities are marked by a different kind of dying: the death of meaning. Despite its crowdedness, many of us live in fear and lonely isolation from those around us; as philosopher Jacques Ellul says, we have lost "the meaning of our neighbor."[8] Our technologies produce better, faster, deadlier machines that rob us of our dignity and disguise us from ourselves and from others. Man is no longer the end to which all our means are directed, but has become the means to other ends. In the city we live in a culture of deception, and it is killing us.

We are deceived by a ubiquitous media that deliberately fabricates false realities that are manipulated to sell advertisers products, maintain networks ratings, and feed its insatiable ego.[9] Television programming debases the individual, preying on viewer's vulnerabilities and effectively reducing human beings to the lowest common denominator. A friend of mine once asked an award winning screen writer what he really thought about the scenes he created. The writer exclaimed, "Its crap, but it sells!" Imagine an industry where people are rewarded handsomely (money, fame, Oscars, Emmys) for producing "crap" and for being really good at pretending to be someone they are not. That is Hollywood of course,

---

8. Here, I am deeply indebted to Jacques Ellul (1912–94), French writer and activist; especially for his ideas pertaining to man's search for meaning, and the impact of technology on humankind. See Ellul, *Presence of the Kingdom*, 125.

9. See Mitroff and Bennis, *The Unreality Industry*, for a thoroughgoing examination of the media's fabrication of reality.

where cosmetic surgery and other modern advances help give actors the appearance of being youthful into their seventies and even eighties.

So called "reality shows," where getting voted off the island is tantamount to getting voted off the planet, are prime indicators of the artificiality of the entertainment industry. To drive this point home, consider NBC's *The Biggest Loser*, which is advertised as a "compelling new weight-loss reality drama in which two celebrity fitness trainers join with top health experts to help overweight contestants transform their bodies, health and ultimately, their lives." If you want to see how fat people are really perceived in our society, tune in with a discerning eye to this compelling new weight loss drama. *Extreme Makeover*, another popular reality program, "follows the stories of the lucky individuals who are chosen for a once-in-a-lifetime chance to be given a truly 'Cinderella like' experience: a real life fairy tale in which their wishes come true, not just by changing their looks, but their lives and destinies."[10] The reviews posted at www.tv.com demonstrate just how disoriented the self has become in this blizzard of falsity. One young viewer writes:

> I need me a extreme makeover I have a body of a 40 yr old and im only 18 please.I wath this show every is season.For some reason i get sadder and sadder with me but happy for your guest.I look at myself every day in the morning in the mirror upset, wondering how i can get on your show.I would be so happy if it was possible. After having a baby and losing my athletic body hurts me so much. I wish there was a way to raise my self esteem. Your show just gives me encouragement to say im not the only one.I would love an extreme makeover it will change my world.I will be so happy if i was on your show.

E! Channel's highly rated reality show, *The Girls Next Door*, depicts the lives of three beautiful women who live at Hugh Hefner's Playboy mansion. The "girls" are filmed from the moment they roll out of bed until they are chauffeured home after a busy schedule, promulgating Hefner's gospel to an adoring public. Naturally, not many of us live next door to the Playboy mansion, or even three beautiful women, and the viewer never sees the essential person behind the voluptuous figures and the blonde

---

10. Descriptions of programming and the posted review (taken verbatim) are from the tv.com. webpage. Accessed January 27, 2008. No pages. Online: http://www.tv.com/extreme-makeover/show/18722/summary.html.

hair. Yet, the portrayals are real enough to convince millions of viewers that they have seen the truth behind the Playboy mystique.

Another insidious factor in the manufacturing of unreality is the escalation of violence in film and television programming. It is difficult to argue that media violence has not had a deleterious effect on our society, especially on our children. Here are some excerpts from a 1999 report of the U.S. Senate Judiciary Committee, which linked media sources to the rise of violent crime:

- By age eighteen, an American child will have seen 16,000 simulated murders and 200,000 acts of violence.
- Television alone is responsible for ten percent of youth violence.
- Modern music lyrics have become increasingly explicit concerning sex, drugs, and violence against women. An average teenager listens to 10,500 hours of rock music during the years between the seventh and twelfth grades.
- Violent video games have an effect on children similar to that of violent television and film. Some experts suggest an even greater pernicious effect, concluding that the violent actions performed in playing video games are more conducive to children's aggression. As one expert concludes, "We're not just teaching kids to kill. We're teaching them to like it."
- According to the Department of Justice, the number of juvenile violent crime arrests in 1997 exceeded the 1988 level by forty-nine percent.[11]

The pervasiveness of media violence has had a numbing effect on our ability to make moral choices; to draw a line in the sand and say, "that's enough!" Day by day, we are slowly being suffocated by violence and the stifling artificiality of urban living in our *postmodern* age.[12] And, like the young woman who needs an "extreme makeover," many Americans have simply lost their way in this culture of deception.

---

11. U.S. Senate Committee on the Judiciary, "Children, Violence and the Media: A Report for Parents and Policy Makers," line 7.

12. I first encountered the term *postmodern* in the writings of philosopher Huston Smith (born 1919). Smith uses the term to distinguish the contemporary world view from the modern mindset, which arose during the seventeenth through nineteenth centuries. See Smith, *Beyond the Postmodern Mind*.

FALSE SELF / TRUE SELF

"Every one of us is shadowed by an illusory person, a *false self*. But, we are not very good at recognizing illusions, least of all the ones we have about ourselves," says Thomas Merton.[13] The genesis of the false self may be traced as far back as infancy, where even the name we are given can begin to mold us into a caricature of someone else. John Smith II is expected to live up to the reputation of John, Sr. and bring honor to the family name. The son of a famous actor or chief executive is measured against the legacy of his father. A young man is pressed to study law, medicine, or dentistry in order to one day take over the family practice. Expectant parents are usually very deliberate in selecting a name for their child, largely because they know the latent power that a name possesses. George Foreman, former heavyweight boxing champion, leveraged his name recognition to the ultimate when he named each of his five sons, "George." While half-a-dozen men named George Foreman at the dinner table can prove interesting, surely each of these Georges has a foot in the door when he applies for a job.

I was named for my grandfather, whom I knew as "Pop." He was well-liked and was regarded as an honest and reputable member of the community. As many young men have done, my father followed his father into a prospering family business. But, for reasons that were never very clear to me, Dad came to dislike his work. Although he discouraged me from taking an interest in his chosen career, he was implacable when it came to my passion for becoming a forest ranger. He insisted that I would attend a college that he approved of, thus following a more "reliable" career path. If I have one regret in my life, it is that I did not follow my heart into the study of forestry. I will never know if I may have missed my deepest calling. Many of you who are reading this understand exactly what I am talking about.

Parental vicariousness often obscures the immature self and channels us into activities that we are not well suited for or have little desire to participate in. Children are automatically enrolled in youth sports when they are as young as four or five. Players who show promise are told that they are going to be the team captain, win the Most Valuable Player award, and get a college scholarship. A coach I know told me of an 18-year old athlete who, when asked about her plans after graduation, informed her

---

13. Merton, *Seeds of Contemplation*, 28.

teammates that she would be attending junior college and then moving on to play softball for one of the premier universities in the country. Yet, this player was not gifted enough to make the starting lineup for her high school team. Unfortunately, no one had ever taken the time to tell her the truth about her skills and opportunities. About one in twenty high school players make it to the collegiate level of athletics, and the odds against earning a spot on a top college sports team are overwhelming. Even in the face of the obvious, parents still persist in promoting false perceptions of who their children are and what they are capable of achieving.

MANY FACES

Through the years, the false self, or *personage*, takes on many faces and employs an assortment of clever disguises.[14] Our manner of dress is one of the more overt indicators of the image we choose to portray. A person's identity is often packaged in an Armani suit, a mink stole, or a Yankee baseball cap: "I'm a stockbroker; I've made it; I'm a winner!"

Look closely at the fashion statements being made by many of today's younger generation. Do boys wear backwards baseball caps to keep the sun off their necks? Do they wear baggy pants that will not stay up because they want to get a suntan on their butts? Of course not! Fashion tells a story and these young males are saying something very revealing, not just about themselves, but about western culture in general. The backwards cap and the droopy britches broadcast: "I am cool. I do not belong to my parents' generation. I have my own crowd." In the 1990s, before the demise of their Oldsmobile line of automobiles, General Motors (GM) made a last-ditch pitch to appeal to the newest generation of drivers. The company advertised the following slogan: "This is not your father's Oldsmobile." The commercial was offensive to older customers, and just like the Oldsmobile brand, it soon went away. But the advertising campaign showed that GM had correctly assessed the nature of youthful rebellion. The cap and the sloppy dress do send a clear message—they are blatant disavowals of traditional masculine responsibility. To receive validation, youths often look to peer groups, which appear—at least on the surface—to have no affinity for conventional mores and practices. Young people clothed in *Gothic* attire, complete with

---

14. Personage is defined as a "dramatic, fictional, or historical character." (Merriam-Webster Online). The term is developed in the writings of Paul Tournier (1898–1986), Swiss psychologist and popular writer. See Tournier, *The Meaning of Persons*.

chains, Mohawk style hairdos, and symbolic body art, demonstrate just how far the self-illusionist will go to exhibit uniqueness. Such eccentric apparel and attention-getting devices help foster "safe zones," where troubled spirits are shielded by the armor of powerful mythologies, medieval sorceries, and transcendent forces.

THE WARRIOR IMAGE

Myth is an important ingredient in the fabrication of the masculine false self, especially myths of the hero, the warrior, and the king. A warrior traditionally paints his body in vibrant colors and pierces his flesh as he prepares for battle. His scars become a "red badge of courage" and attest to his strength in vanquishing his enemies. In ancient times, victorious warriors were feted as heroes and were handsomely rewarded when they returned home from successful military campaigns. Nowadays, the hero myth is strikingly replayed in popular culture's caricature of the warrior—the professional athlete. Not unlike their predecessors who once battled in the Coliseum in ancient Rome, modern day "gladiators," with names like *Golden State Warriors* and *Oakland Raiders*, still take to the arena in grand spectacles. But instead of wearing the heavy armor of old, contemporary sporting participants are recognized by the names and numbers worn on their team jerseys. Athletes are well aware that numbers, like names, symbolize tradition, convey power, and project imagery. When a great athlete's career is finished, sports teams immortalize him by retiring his number and hanging his jersey from the arena's rafters.

The sports uniform is a convenient layer of self-identity protection, and it is not just players who wear them. In recent decades, sales of expensive apparel and memorabilia have skyrocketed as fans seek to emulate their athletic heroes. As an example, the National Basketball Association (NBA) reported that the 2005 NBA playoffs resulted in a 150 percent jump in sales of *Phoenix Suns* merchandise, with star player Steve Nash's jersey tripling in revenues.[15] While few are paid at the level of a sports professional, an authentic looking jersey can help a fan look the part of a star and identify with a winning team.

Many contemporary sports figures use body art to proliferate the legend of the warrior. Tattoos, which require submission to a certain level of pain, have become today's badge of courage. For example, tattoos ad-

---

15. National Basketball Association, "Surging Merchandise," para. 3.

vertising "Superman," "Chosen1," and "Dynasty Raider" adorn the fleshed canvases of leading NBA stars Shaquille O'Neal, Lebron James, and Allen Iverson. Body art is a personal narrative that tells of the struggles and the triumphs in a man's life. They are outward expressions of the deep feelings that arise from personal relationships and formative experiences along the way. Tattoos have also become a type of validation, boldly advertising the image that players have of themselves and wish to be recognized by.

As part of commercial human packaging, actors, musicians, and other performers in the entertainment industry frequently adopt new names. Self styled artists and entertainers benefit from these pseudonyms in several important ways. Having multiple names is a way to compartmentalize one's public and private life. A man can cast off the baggage that comes with a primary name's history; the "new man" is liberated from the dark shadows and bitter memories of his past. Another name offers a chance for a fresh start, permitting individuals to personally design their caricature of the perfect person—designer bodies, designer wardrobe, designer persons. Elective cosmetic surgery has become a popular means for men and women to re-package themselves behind the appearance of youth and beauty. Procedures like botox, tummy tucks, and breast augmentation have escalated to epidemic proportions in the western world, and are fast becoming an international phenomenon. In 2003, *The Boston Globe* reported how this widening trend is impacting the Far East, especially China, where many women seek to tap into the power of pulchritude. One woman reports that her appearance has changed so completely that she must now celebrate two birthdays—the original one and the date of her first cosmetic surgery. A prominent Chinese surgeon says that he prefers doing elective cosmetic surgeries because, "I love to create things of beauty. It is a gift to the world."[16] Note that the doctor dispassionately refers to his patients as "things of beauty," rather than as persons. Cosmetic surgery has become like a sophisticated version of the Mr. Potato Head toy; irrespective of what the potato comes out to look like after its makeover, at its core it is still a spud. Sadly, the passage to a new identity often results in disappointment and disillusionment for these crossover individuals.

The development of the illusory self may have reached its zenith in the pop music industry, where performers adopt flamboyant monikers

---

16. Freiss, "China grows beholden to skin-deep beauty," line 60.

and appear in "high shock" videos. Ricardo Brown, who calls himself a "gangsta grappa," becomes "Kurupt the Kingpin" (evil ruler), or "Young Gotti" (Mafia type). "Ice Cube" is a very cool name for one successful American rapper, whose real name is O'Shea Jackson. "Snoop Dog," formerly "Snoop Doggy Dog," is really Cordozar Calvin Broadus, Jr. A look into their backgrounds quickly reveals why these men changed their names and assumed new identities.

Singers and musicians who are not gifted enough to make a name for themselves in the prevailing entertainment establishment simply create new genres of unreality—music niches like "rap," "electronica," "punk," and "screamo." Though they lack much *bona fidé* talent as entertainers, jet-setters like Paris Hilton call themselves actors or artists, and command media attention, owing almost exclusively to their fabulous wealth and extravagant lifestyles. Abetting the magnification of these personalities are reporters and a bold new generation of photographers called paparazzi, who relentlessly pursue celebrities in hopes of cashing-in with just the right shot.

Our infatuation with professional athletes, musicians, and Hollywood actors is linked to our deep psychological need to establish a meaningful self-image. But as we are molded into the shape of someone else, we move farther and farther from who we once were. This abstraction creates a "split personality"—the person we are and the person we are not. This is the portrait of the false self that Thomas Merton painted through his many writings. The false self is but a chimera of the person that God formed at our inception. When a man seeks out his true self, he begins to realign himself with the Creation. In the process, he may even rediscover his calling. Merton well knew this and he has given us a simple, thought provoking illustration of the way Nature reveals her secrets of authenticity.

> A tree gives glory to God first of all by being a tree. For in being what God means it to be, it is imitating an idea which is in God and which is not distinct from the essence of God, and therefore a tree imitates God by being a tree.
>
> The more it is like itself, the more it is like Him. If it tried to be like something else which it was never intended to be, it would be less like God and therefore it would give him less glory.
>
> But there is something more. No two trees are alike. And their individuality is no imperfection. On the contrary: the perfection

of each created thing is not merely in its conformity to an abstract type but in its own individuality with itself. This particular tree will give glory to God by spreading out its roots in the earth and raising its branches into the air and the light in a way that no other tree before or after it ever did or will do.[17]

Merton must have been standing in the company of trees, immersed in their wisdom, as he made this penetrating observation. How few places remain where a man can see beyond our phantom world of shadows and into the land of infinite wilderness!

Rattlesnakes and bears and trees are the truest of teachers. They are habitually themselves; never anything other than what they were meant to be. This is the lesson that each one of us must learn. When we seek authenticity, as modeled by the creatures of the wilderness, we once again discover the trail home.

Lessons of the Wild

- *Self-awareness:* "I am truly alive and I have a wild heart!"
- *Humility:* "I am part of something much bigger."
- *Faith:* "I am not alone."
- *Tolerance:* "All of life is beautiful."
- *Hope:* "Life is abundant with new opportunities."
- *Honesty:* "I am going to die!"

---

17. Merton, *Seeds of Contemplation*, 24.

5

Passages

I wouldn't give a fig for the simplicity on this side of complexity, but I would give everything for the simplicity on the other side of complexity.

—Oliver Wendell Holmes

Not long ago, I was contacted by a single father who was excited by important developments regarding his twelve-year old son. Since the divorce four years before, Daniel's son, Nikos, had been living with his mother, but made it very clear to everyone that he wanted to live with his Dad. Nikos moved in with Daniel, who anticipates spending more quality time with his son, especially during this formative time of his life. Daniel remembered that I was a fisherman and wanted to talk about Nikos's sudden interest in flyfishing. "I really can't explain it," he said. "I never did any fishing as a boy, but Nikos has a keen interest in becoming a fly fisherman. He has been bringing home fishing books from the library and studying about insects and fly tying. He already knows a lot about it, and he's been after me to take him fishing. Frankly, I don't know the first thing about what equipment to buy or where to go. Can you help me out?"

Nikos is a perceptive boy who knows that he is standing at the threshold of manhood. He has known for a long time that his father should be his guide on this once in a lifetime journey. When he was just five years old, Nikos gave Daniel assurances of this when he declared, "I chose you in heaven." The boy's passion for activities like flyfishing is not surprising. He often accompanies his Dad on hiking trips to the local mountains, and in 2002 they had a benchmark experience on a vacation to Park City, Utah. They now return each winter, in what has become their special pilgrimage together. Something about these adventures has kindled Nikos's interest in being with his father in the outdoors. Likewise, Daniel has begun to blossom in his role as a mentor and guide. Father and son are embarking on an epic journey that will change them both. Each, in his individual way, is sure to discover something of the sublime relationship between the natural world and the wilderness of the inner spirit.

Like the rest of the boys of his generation, Nikos is facing one of life's most difficult changes. At this time of life, a boy needs a trusted leader who has earnestly fathomed the depths of his soul and who understands the longings of his true heart. In the quest to discover his masculine identity, Nikos must be guided by a man who has had the courage to confront his demons—a man who has already come face-to-face with the Great Spirit and learned his sacred name.

Inside every boy is a yearning—a wildness—that seeks its expression in wild places. Unfortunately, many young men will not have the opportunity to experience Nature as Nikos has. Fewer and fewer boys are blessed with a conscientious guide like Daniel to lead them through the process of initiation. For his part, Daniel's assignment is to find the right trailhead and be able to recognize the ducks along the way. This can be a daunting task for a young father, but there will be other men to come alongside him to support and encourage him as he welcomes his son into the company of men. It would be well if Daniel enlists a few duckbuilders among this supporting cast of male mentors. These men of wisdom can make all the difference.

FROM PLACE TO PERSONHOOD

Borrowing from the words of May Sarton: "Childhood is a place, as well as a time."[1] We anticipate that by a certain age—hopefully, by their early twenties—our offspring will move from the place that is childhood into the fullness of becoming an adult. This passage is the first of the two great life-changing events. It is the movement outward and into the public square—the time when a boy longs to discover how he fits in with the

---

1. Quote unsourced.

world around him. There are milestones along the way, and every culture has its own form of recognition. Native American and other tribal peoples mark this movement through ceremonial male initiation rites. In the ancient Hebrew tradition, when a Jewish boy turns thirteen he is feted with a *bar mitzvah*, acknowledging his responsibilities to the laws of the Torah. In like fashion, customs like birthday parties and graduation ceremonies celebrate markers on the way to adulthood.

The second great life-changing event takes place much later in our journey. It is inevitable, beginning in our middle years and culminating at the place called "old age." This passage is complex, usually accompanied by declining health, diminishing activity, and a dwindling circle of family and friends. Whereas the passage from boyhood to manhood is a journey outward, the passage to old age is an inward one. It presents us with an opportunity for a reawakening of our hidden gifts; a reflective time, nurtured by a sense of overall perspective granted only by the accumulation of years. Old age is the time and place where we may finally discover who we are as persons. It can, and should, become the fulfillment of our unique personhood.[2]

Carl Jung proposed that we pass through certain "cultural phases" during our lives. Early on, we are trained in a decidedly collective culture, wherein we are oriented toward production and achievement. This period of life is characterized by individual specialization, establishing a high degree of refinement in relatively limited fields. We necessarily leverage our education and learned skills to compete in the marketplace and optimize our earning power. The metrics for success become accumulated wealth, material possessions, and social status. A common byproduct of this age of specialization, however, is the sublimation of some of our richest endowments. In the drive toward success and prosperity we often stifle the development of self, failing to adequately explore the full breadth of our gifts and talents. But in the second phase of life, says Jung, we can begin to unlock the "values of personality . . . and grasp intelligently the meaning of individual life."[3] These latter years can become an *age of wisdom*—the time of life when men and women no longer need external validation;

---

2. Many of my thoughts on personhood are gleaned from Paul Tournier, whose insights into the human person are exceptional. See Tournier, *The Meaning of Persons*, and *The Whole Person in a Broken World*. Tournier was deeply influenced by the life and work of Carl Jung (1875–1961), who is generally considered to be the founder of analytical psychology.

3. Tournier, *Learning to Grow Old*, 11.

and by virtue of their cumulative experiences, are poised to make unique contributions for the betterment of the rest of us.

In *Leadership Is an Art*, Max DePree relates an episode that illustrates the way in which specialization and economic necessity can prompt us to conceal our diverse gifts. DePree's father, D. J. DePree, was the founder and president of the Herman Miller Furniture Company at a time when factories were run, not by advanced technologies, but by steam engines powered by boilers. The chief overseer of the factory's mechanical operations was called a "millwright." One day Herman Miller's millwright died, and the senior DePree, who was then a young manager, went to the home of the grieving widow to pay his respects. After a few awkward moments, the woman asked if she could read some poetry to him. DePree politely agreed. When she had finished reading, he remarked that the poetry was very good. When he asked her who wrote it, he was surprised to find out that it had been the millwright. The obvious question arises: "Was the deceased man a poet who did millwright's work, or was he a millwright who wrote poetry?"[4]

This is a question that begs other questions: Are we on the trail toward discovering our authentic personhood? Are we exercising our talents in a way that affirms our deep calling? What will be our legacy when we are gone?

TRANSITIONS

While there are but two major passages to be made on our pilgrimage to wholeness as persons, we also face many other formidable obstacles on our life's journey. In negotiating these obstacles we pass through periods of change, which are commonly referred to as "transitions." For bears and other animals, transitions are instinctual and are dictated by the seasons. In the fall, a bear senses that his life is about to change, and for an animal who must consume more than twenty thousand calories per day in preparation for hibernation, the search for food becomes an obsession. Soon enough though, the bear's metabolism begins to wind down and he retreats to his den, where he spends the winter months. As spring makes its appearance, so does the bear; emerging from his long slumber to renew the perennial cycle of bruin life.

For humans, transitions are much more complicated. A marriage, the birth of a child, a promotion at work, or moving to a new home are events

---

4. DePree, *Leadership is an Art*, 6.

that can dramatically alter the way we manage our affairs. Such lifestyle shifts create excitement and usually result in positive outcomes, but not all transitions are welcome ones. A divorce, the loss of a job, or the death of a loved one are major events that can have a telling impact on us, effectively eroding the joys of living. But if we are to maintain a holistic well-being—body, mind, and spirit—we must find ways of negotiating these blockages on the trail. It is never easy to make radical departures from old ways, and some people are more successful than others in making transitions, ultimately leading to happier, healthier, and more fulfilling lives. Successful transitioners seem to draw on reserves of inner strength during times of significant change, whereas people lacking in this "personal power" are poorly equipped to deal with the challenges of change, often becoming scarred for life. What is personal power, where does it come from, and how can Nature play a role in its discovery and development?

Janet Hagberg is a leadership consultant and healer who has spent much of her professional career in examining the sources of our strength during the different stages of our lives. Some years ago I had the opportunity to talk with Hagberg about her critically acclaimed book, *Real Power: Stages of Personal Power in Organizations*, which was written during the aftermath of her helping a friend through a time of crisis. Her friend was highly successful in the corporate world and was in complete control of her affairs, until things began to unravel. Her husband abruptly left her for someone else, then family illness and death sent her into a tailspin. As Hagberg supported this woman, she came to the startling realization that she too was in the midst of transition. It was this "crisis of movement" that gave her the inspiration to both discover what constitutes personal power and to write a book about it.

Hagberg defines personal power as, "the extent to which one is able to link the outer capacity for action (external power) with the inner capacity for reflection (internal power)."[5] She identifies six stages:

1. Powerlessness—lacking self-esteem, trapped, uninformed
2. Power by association—apprentice, learning, new self-awareness
3. Power by symbols—the control stage, ambitious, dynamo
4. Power by reflection—reflective, confused, having influence, strong

---

5. Hagberg, *Real Power*, xvii. For further insight, see resources online at: http://www.janethagberg.com/.

5. Power by purpose—inner vision, self-accepting, confident of life calling
6. Power by *Gestalt*[6]—self-sacrifice, powerless, "souls of the earth"

In Hagberg's model, the stages of personal power are attained sequentially, each stage being marked by a *crisis of movement*—giving up something familiar in order to be able to move to the next stage. In thinking about my meeting with Janet Hagberg, I was surprised at how neatly my life's journey fit within the *Real Power* model. It was easy to see how bogged down I had become in the symbols of success—my home, my automobile, the way I dressed, and so on. I recalled my encounter with the "Presence" on the Kern River, remembering how the "Power of the Slowing" had coaxed me into an ultra-reflective state. Leading up to that moment, I had thought mainly in generalities about the meaning of my life. But now, I saw that Nature had acted as a catalyst, channeling my thinking and pointing me in the direction of a purposeful life. My revelation in the middle of the Kern was the turning point in my movement from a life measured by external symbols to one of assessment and reflection. I arrived in Nature, afflicted and confused; I left reassured and focused, certain that my life had not yet fulfilled its full promise. Like others before me, I too had seen a vision in the wild.

A few months passed, and then one day out of the blue, I received a phone call from a friend who told me about a job opportunity that matched my career interests. Ironically, I had interviewed with the firm's general manager a year earlier for a similar position, but was not selected. This time things were different. I had changed so much in the intervening months that the manager could not even remember me from our previous meeting. Before I knew it, I was employed in the career consulting field, assisting men and women who were between jobs. My colleagues were extraordinary people, and I witnessed the dedication and the earnest compassion they had for our clients. I shared in their jubilation as new employment turned clients' uncertainties and fears into joy and hopefulness. I collaborated with human resources directors and senior managers in dealing with company downsizings, employee morale issues, and leadership problems. I found that I was making a measurable difference

---

6. Ibid., 129. Gestalt is "like being in a balloon that is circling above the earth and making occasional landings. People in Gestalt see the whole picture; they radiate peace and calm, courage and wisdom."

in people's lives. My vision seen in the wilderness had become a reality. I had found my higher calling.

VISIONS IN THE WILD

One of the key lessons of male initiation, "Your life is not about you," resonates with me when I think of this chapter of my life. For six years following my Kern River epiphany I prospered in my sales and consulting career, reaching personal benchmarks that I never could have imagined. I learned firsthand that Nature's wisdom can be applied to help sustain us, even in the most difficult of times. In fact, it is often during our darkest days that her voice rises above the chaos of anger, frustration, and despair. Mine is but one of countless tales of people in transition who experienced Nature's healing power and who ultimately found their redemption in the wilderness. Among these truly unique stories is one told passionately—almost reverently—by a most unusual stranger. What makes this man's journey so compelling is the way in which he discovered his calling and how his life intersected with two very unlikely candidates for a life-altering experience in the world of Nature.

Was it by chance—or destiny—that first brought us together on a rainy afternoon in a Pasadena, California bookshop? A shop employee and I were reminiscing about our hiking adventures in the San Gabriel Mountains, when a rugged looking man who had been standing nearby approached us and declared, "I have had a lot of amazing experiences in the mountains!" He introduced himself as Cort Heibert. Then, at our urging, he proceeded to relate one of the most astonishing accounts of personal transformation that I have ever heard.

The wilderness always held a powerful attraction for Hiebert, whose adventuresome spirit often led him into close encounters with danger. When he was nineteen years old, he and his younger sister, Suzy, embarked on a self-guided float trip through the Boquillas Canyon section of the Rio Grande River along the border between Texas and Mexico. What began as a spontaneous weekend adventure became a nightmare that would forever change the course of their lives. The teens were enjoying the panoramic scenery of the Class II rapids when their raft suddenly sprung a leak. They were able to maneuver out of the fast water and eventually guided the crippled craft to the river bank. By now it was already late in the afternoon. Cort and Suzy determined that their best chance for survival lay in crossing the remote wilderness area on foot. Boquillas Canyon is surrounded by desert; inhospitable terrain without water, marked trails, or shelter from the fierce winds. They received little comfort from the name given to an imposing hurdle that lay in their path, infamously known as the Dead Horse Mountains. The only provisions they had were two quarts of water, a couple of candy bars, a map, and a pocket knife. For warmth and protection, Cort wisely cut up a section of the raft and slung it over his shoulder as they prepared to leave.

Not many adventurers have attempted to traverse the Dead Horse Mountains on foot, especially when as ill-prepared as these two young people were. Undaunted, they struck out over the desert in the general direction of a main road marked on the map. That night the winds became so violent that Suzy and Cort were forced to wedge themselves tightly into a narrow cleft in the cliffs, shielded only by the raft. When the sun came up the next morning they were already weary from their struggles against the elements. But knowing the fate awaiting them if they could not make it through the mountains, they pressed on. As they fought against the persistent winds, Cort was blown off the edge of a hillside and into an ocotillo cactus, sustaining numerous puncture wounds. By the third day, he was too weak to continue. Having gone more than twenty-four hours without water and having been sapped of his strength due to the severity of his injuries, Cort lay down and told his sister that he was going to die, demanding she go on without him. Suzy reluctantly left, vowing to find help and return as soon as possible. It was not long, however, before she returned and excitedly told Cort that she had seen what looked like a road not far ahead. Perhaps it was just a mirage, but they had to find out. Suzy, forced to kick and shake him out of his lethargic condition, was finally able to get Cort to his feet, and together they trudged to the crest of a small rise. As they scanned the desert floor below them, they saw a shiny streak blazing across the sand. It was an automobile. In a short time they made it to the road, where they were soon picked up by a Winnebago motor home and driven to a National Park campsite.

The Heiberts recovered from their miraculous ordeal, but they were never the same. Cort was often seen in the company of society's misfits and down-and-outs—addicts, derelicts, and runaways—helping them to find a way out from their brokenness. Suzy's worldview had been turned upside-down. Prior to her experience on the Rio Grande, Suzy was an avowed atheist, but afterwards she converted to Christianity and became active in church and community outreach. During their time in the desert, brother and sister had together learned two valuable lessons: "I am not alone," and "I am part of something much bigger." The Hiebert's had heard the still small voices of the wild and they responded fervently to their callings in service to their fellow human beings. Both will tell you that what happened in the Texas desert was no accident. They are certain that, as they walked through the valley of the shadow of death, they were being led by a deep abiding Presence.

Some years later, Cort Hiebert was in the construction business, managing a renovation project in south central Los Angeles. As the home turf for two deadly street gangs, the Crips and the Bloods, this area of southern California was considered a very dangerous place to be, especially for an outsider like Cort Hiebert. One afternoon in a remote part of the jobsite, he was confronted by a bulky, threatening looking stranger. Fearing the worst, Cort haltingly asked the man what he wanted. "I have just gotten out of prison. I'm a killer. I have killed more than twenty men," was the man's blunt reply. Before Cort could respond, the stranger caught him by complete surprise when he asked, "Do you have any work?" Cort thought for a moment and then offered a part-time job to the ex-convict, who gave his name as "Nardy."

Each weekend, Cort retreated to the mountains in his four-wheel drive truck to get away from the city. One Friday afternoon, as he was packing up for the week, Nardy asked him where he was going. When Cort explained that he was bound for the high country, Nardy asked if he could tag along. That was just fine with Cort. As they traveled towards the mountains, Cort learned that Nardy's real name was Oscar. His story was stereotypical of young men growing up in the inner city. Born to an unwed mother living on welfare, Oscar never knew his father and had no positive male role models while growing up. With no supervision or guidance, and with dim prospects for the future, Oscar naturally turned to gangs for validation. He was quickly sucked into the maelstrom of gang life, eventually landing in prison.

When the two men reached the bumpy dirt road that led upwards into the national forest, Cort shifted into four-wheel drive, and the truck began its rugged ascent. They were within a half-mile or so of the crest, when Oscar turned pale and abruptly demanded that Cort stop the truck. "I have never been afraid of anything in my life," he said, "but I'm scared shitless right now." His first time on Nature's turf and completely unnerved by the narrowness of the road cut into the steep mountainside, Oscar could go no further. Cort advised him to get out and walk the rest of the way. Oscar readily complied. It was not long before he reached the top, where he sat down on a large rock that commanded a panoramic view of the valley below. After a few minutes, Cort approached him and asked if he was alright. Oscar mumbled a few words, which revealed the narrowness of his world: "I never knew this was here. I never knew . . ." Cort recalls, "In that instant, Oscar changed. I can't describe it. He had a different look on his face. From then on, he seemed like a new man. He stopped doing drugs and stayed employed. He led a pretty normal life, for as long as I knew him."

A man does a lot of thinking in prison. But a six by eight cell is no place to gain perspective; it is no place to grasp the context of one's life. Visions are seen from high places. Never before had Oscar sat at Nature's knee. Never was he taught the essential lesson of the wild—*I am truly alive and I have a wild heart!* He knew much of his wildness, of course, but he was never truly alive. Gangs and prisons are places, not of life, but of death and decay. The view from the mountaintop gave Oscar his first glimpse of beauty; it was probably the first time that he had ever experienced anything that was pure and good.

Looking back at Janet Hagberg's model of personal power, it is easy to see that men like Oscar are stuck in Stage 1 (Powerlessness). Despite his imposing physical appearance and gang affiliation, Oscar lacked any real power. He was empty inside—fearful, dependent, and utterly bereft of the resources necessary to grow to his potential as a human person. He was misdirected on the trail of life, without a map or a compass, and without hope. Oscar began to move to Stage 2 (Power by Association) as he spent time with Cort Hiebert (Stage 5: Power by Purpose). Cort's integrity and personal example demonstrated to Oscar that real men live for something beyond themselves. It should come as no surprise to the reader of this book that Nature played such a pivotal role in Oscar's surprising transformation.

A few days after we first met, Cort phoned me and explained that there was more to tell about his wilderness experiences. "I have to tell you about a hooker that I once took to the mountains," he said. My curiosity was piqued when we got together the following week. Cort began, "One time, I was having breakfast at a local restaurant before setting out on a five-day camping trip. I couldn't help but notice a young woman seated at a nearby table, who by all appearances was a prostitute. She looked like she was down on her luck, so I asked her if she wanted something to eat, and she joined me at my table. When she asked me where I was going, I explained that I was going camping for a few days in the local mountains. Then, I blurted out, 'Wanna go?'" They must have made a curious pair that evening as they sat by the campfire—a wilderness evangelist and a hooker dressed in high heels and dime store jewelry.

For several days, Cort and the young woman just talked, while Nature worked her magic. The woman had many questions about Heibert's family, his attraction to Nature, and his faith in a higher power. She offered him sex, but it wasn't sex that he wanted. When they returned to the city, the woman confessed, "I don't want to go back to the streets." Cort offered to let her stay in his rented room for a few days until she could make other arrangements. He returned from work one day to find her neatly dressed and packed to leave. "I need one more favor," she said. "Need some money?" he asked. "No, I need a ride to the bus station," was her response. When asked about her destination, she calmly replied, "I've made peace with my family. I'm going home." Cort drove the woman to a Greyhound bus station and said goodbye. He never saw her again.

When he returned to the motel, he picked up a tattered Bible that the ex-hooker had left on the table. When he opened it, he found its pages teeming with notes and reflections—the tracks of a seeker in an uncharted land. From the markings, it was obvious that certain passages, especially those dealing with genealogy and family relationships, had been read many times over. Day after day, in the solitude of the motel room, the woman pondered her brokenness—her separation from those whom she loved. Then she chose to begin rebuilding her fractured life. Just as the evangelist and the murderer had done, the prostitute found hope in the wilderness.

LOSING A DREAM

It is not only for people like the characters above that the city can become a place of broken dreams and forlorn hopes. In one form or another, urban living exacts its toll on everyone. When we hear someone say, "I'm going camping or hiking or fishing or mountain climbing for a few days to get away from it all, to unwind," what are they really saying? They are admitting that they are worn out by the demands made on them at home and at the office. They are wearied of meetings, deadlines, and reports. Their lives have become jaded by the superficialities of a steel and concrete world. They have lost the texture of life's meaning. Consciously or not, they hope to recapture that sense of wonder that makes life worth living. Such people are looking for clarity and a sense of perspective. They long to see the view from the top.

Every one of us needs a vision for our lives—a preferred future that can leverage who we really are for the maximum benefit of everyone around us. Nature opens our eyes; she is our window to eternity. Our future is informed and inspired by the lessons we learn in Nature's world:

- *Self-awareness*
- *Humility*
- *Faith*
- *Tolerance*
- *Hope*
- *Honesty*

But when a man loses his dream, he loses his capacity to see the road ahead; he loses himself. Missing in so many lives is a child's innocence and the hope that life has a purpose. Without a compelling vision, we become like a sailing ship on a listless sea—dead in the water.

During the late 1990s, I belonged to a small group of men who met weekly to discuss issues of importance like personal relationships, work, faith, world affairs, and the like. A man named Roger was invited to join our "Wednesday Group" and he quickly became the focus of many of our conversations. A graduate of Stanford University, Roger was bright and affable, seemingly destined to follow in his father's footsteps and someday take over the family business. But Roger found it difficult to work with his father and decided to pursue a teaching career instead. Somewhere along the way he took the wrong trail and began drinking heavily. By the time we came to know him, he had become a hopeless alcoholic.

During one of our meetings, Roger made a statement that I shall never forget. The topic was death and the incomparable sense of loss that accompanies the final departure of someone dear to us. I was sharing the impact that my father's death had on me when Roger interjected, "Losing a parent is hard, but what happens when you lose your dream?" The room was silent. No had an immediate response to Roger's question, but each of us heard the pervading sadness underlying his words—the sorrow that summed up his life.

Roger's excessive drinking was having a devastating effect on his family and he was losing touch with the people who meant the most to him. Intimacy with his wife was non-existent. His son had lost all respect for him, and as the months wore on, Roger's mentally-challenged daughter was becoming more and more reclusive. The members of our small group made every effort to convince him that he was on the road to oblivion, and each attempted in his own way to help, but it was to no avail. For my part, I once drove him several hours away and checked him into a well-known rehabilitation center for men in Palm Springs, California. He lasted a few days, before sneaking out and hitchhiking back to the Los Angeles area. I had to admit that I was losing patience with Roger, who declined to deal with his addiction in any constructive way.

At one of our meetings I suggested to him that he accompany me on a day trip to the Kern River. Something told me that if I could get Roger up into the mountains, then he might see things differently. It was beginning to look like a bad idea when I picked him up at his home at 5:00 A.M. Roger was dressed like he was going downtown instead of on a hiking trip. He explained that he had never been in the outdoors much and the business clothes and cheap tennis shoes were all he had to wear.

Four hours later, we had finished our breakfast at Cheryl's Diner in Kernville. We then drove twenty miles upriver to the Johnsondale Bridge parking lot, locked the car, and started up the familiar Kern River trail. We were having a pleasant conversation, when suddenly I realized that I had forgotten to tell Roger something very important. When I announced that we were in rattlesnake country, he stopped cold in his tracks and muttered: "Rattlesnakes . . . no I couldn't handle seeing a rattlesnake. I'm deathly afraid of snakes." I explained that we were unlikely to see one, and anyway we were not far from our destination, so we might as well keep going. You can pretty well guess what happened next. Not more than a few hundred yards ahead, I surprised a sizeable rattler sunning itself in the dry grass along the trail. I did not immediately see the snake, but I heard its unmistakable greeting. As it coiled to strike, I surged forward, leaving Roger and me separated by the angry serpent. The trail was cut into a steep granite hillside, and with the sheer drop off to the river, we had nowhere to go. Obviously shaken, Roger asked me what we should do. Perhaps a bit selfishly, I told him that we had come a long way and I hoped to wet my fly line to see if I could raise a trout or two. I offered to toss the car keys to him so he could return to the car and wait for me there. He asked what other options he had. Somewhat cavalierly I replied, "Well, if the snake settles down and uncoils, you can jump over it."

It was a foolish suggestion. Imagine a sixty-something, out-of-shape city slicker in cheap tennies jumping over a venomous snake on a narrow precipice. "Can't happen," you say? Well, it did! After a few minutes, as if right on cue, the snake uncoiled and lay still at the edge of the trail. Roger steadied his nerve, then skipped forward and leapt as far as he could. He managed to just clear the snake, successfully completing the most dangerous feat he had ever attempted. The trout fishing was below par, but Roger's conquest made our day.

I lost track of him for some years thereafter, until we met unexpectedly at the home of a mutual friend. "Roger, how the heck are you?" I asked. "Great," he said. "I have been sober for six years and I have you to thank for much of it." I was honored, but not sure what he meant. "Remember when you took me to the Kern River, and we had that encounter with the rattlesnake?" Who could forget it, I thought. "Well that was perhaps the biggest turning point of my life. Jumping over that snake is the metaphor for overcoming my addiction to alcohol." I fought back tears as he went on to describe the importance of the events of that memorable day. Roger has rebuilt his relationships with his family and friends; gone are most of the fears and broken dreams. Although he will always be "in recovery," Roger is happy and is making every effort to lead the life he was made for.

Nature's transformations are more than just stories in a book about people you will never meet. They are real events and they can happen to any one of us. We all are broken in some way; we all need restoration. Every human being who has ever lived has had pains, hurts, and unfulfilled dreams. But losing a dream does not have to mean that we have come to the end of our trail. Visions can still be seen in the wilderness—at the top of a mountain, in the currents of a river ... *and in the depths of our souls.*

LOOKING ON THE INTERIOR

Parker Palmer writes beautifully about vision in a book named after an old Quaker saying. In *Let Your Life Speak*, Palmer notes: "What a long time it can take to become the person one has always been! How often in the process we mask ourselves in faces that are not our own. How much dissolving and shaking of ego we must endure before we discover our deep identity—the true self within every human being that is the seed of authentic vocation."[7] There is a hidden person inside each one of us, shrouded in mystery and disguised beneath the cloak of pride and ego. Quakers refer to this hidden self as the "inner light." If a man pulls back the curtain of his soul, he reveals this inner light—the bright essence of whom God created once upon a time. Throughout the book, Palmer poses an unsettling question: "Are you living the life that wants to live in you?" Are we allowing our inner light to radiate outward, illuminating the way ahead and brightening the lives of others? Have we fairly accepted our limitations and sought to discover our potentialities? What is our vision for ourselves? Where, and to what, is our calling?

The simple elegance of Palmer's writing portrays his genuine humility and his openness to an honest self-appraisal. He writes freely of his "journey into darkness" in his battle with clinical depression, and of several months spent in "the snakepit of the soul." Palmer reveals Nature's restorative influence in his life; of the significance of his escapes into the wilds of the Boundary Waters on the border between Minnesota and Ontario, Canada. He describes the "hidden wholeness of all things," clues to which can be found in the staunch presence of the jack pine tree. Palmer alludes to an absolutely stunning poem by William Stafford:

> *Some time when the river is ice ask me mistakes I have made. Ask me whether what I have done is my life. Others have come in their slow way into my thought and some have tried to help or to hurt: ask me what difference their strongest love or hate has made.*
>
> *I will listen to what you say. You and I can turn and look at the silent river and wait. We know the current is there, hidden; and there are comings and goings from miles away that hold the stillness exactly before us. What the river says, that is what I say*[8]

The spirit of the river flows into the soul of the seeker who ventures into the magical world of wilderness. Visions are seen in the comings and goings of the incessant currents. Knowledge of the sacred comes to those familiar with the silence and the stillness. And the river speaks to them with the language of integrity. What does the river say, you ask? The river whispers the same words as the tree: "I am here! I am here! I am life, eternal life."

7. Palmer, *Let Your Life Speak*, 9.
8. Stafford, *The Way It Is*, 56.

There is a beautiful old Zen saying that goes something like this:

> Before I grasped Zen, the mountains were nothing but mountains and the rivers nothing but rivers. When I got Zen, the mountains were no longer mountains and the rivers no longer rivers. But when I understood Zen, the mountains were only mountains and the rivers only rivers.[9]

One finds an uncomplicated meaning behind these seemingly mysterious words. The Buddhist understanding of life derives from the same fount of wisdom that prompted Oliver Wendell Holmes to say, "I wouldn't give a fig for the simplicity on this side of complexity, but I would give everything for the simplicity on the other side of complexity."[10] These words are not cryptic; one does not have to be able to decipher hieroglyphics or read tea leaves to break the code. Life is far simpler than we try to make it out to be. The first step toward true happiness lies in discovering who we really are—our true self. The passage to wholeness requires courage and is often painful, but the simplicity of being authentic is worth the effort.

Lessons of the Wild

- *Self-awareness:* "I am truly alive and I have a wild heart!"
- *Humility:* "I am part of something much bigger."
- *Faith:* "I am not alone."
- *Tolerance:* "All of life is beautiful."
- *Hope:* "Life is abundant with new opportunities."
- *Honesty:* "I am going to die!"

---

9. Merton, *Zen and the Birds of Appetite*, 140.

10. The Supreme Court Historical Society, "History of the Court: Timeline of the Justices, Oliver Wendell Holmes, Jr." para. 1. Oliver Wendell Holmes was a Civil War veteran, who was wounded three times in the conflict; later, he graduated from Harvard University Law School. In 1902, he was appointed by President Theodore Roosevelt to the Supreme Court of the United States, where he served as an Associate Justice for twenty-nine years.

6

Crossing the Abyss

To speak of wilderness is to speak of wholeness.

—Gary Snyder

ONE CAN ONLY IMAGINE the sense of adventure that must have stirred the hearts of Spanish explorers like Hernan Cortez and Ponce de Leon as they sailed westward to the wilds of the Americas in search of golden cities and fountains of youth. The pride of achievement in being first—the very first to fly solo across the great ocean, to stand atop the highest pinnacle, to straddle the axis of the globe—surely provided a powerful impetus for the wilderness exploits of Charles Lindbergh, Sir Edmund Hillary, and Captain Robert E. Peary. What drove these men? What were they really after? Could it have been something beyond the desire for fame and fortune that fueled their improbable journeys?

While riches and recognition by our fellows may seem to be primary motivations, clues found in our human DNA suggest that we are in pursuit of something less tangible, but something that is vastly more important, as we travel the trails of life. Thomas Merton saw this clearly when he queried, "What can we gain by sailing to the moon if we are not able to cross the abyss that separates us from ourselves?"[1] Since we first arrived on the earthly scene, nothing about our nature has changed, except for perhaps the way we think about ourselves. We men of today are as we always have been; possessing the selfsame attributes, needs, and drivers as our ancestors—physiologically, psychologically and spiritually. Whether we are much aware of it or not, man is still driven by the yearning to know who he is and to notch his place in the cosmos. Like Cortez, Lindbergh, Muir, Schweitzer, and the pantheon of heroes who blazed the trail, we too are on a great quest. *We are men in search of our souls!*

Everyone is looking for something deeper in their lives, but few of us are able to articulate exactly what that "something" is. Seldom will you hear someone say, "Oh yeah! The reason that I do what I do is so that I can find my soul." Yet, beneath it all, we dream of finding meaning in our personal relationships and in our myriad activities. *We want to discover our joy!*

As we have already seen, some of us lose the dream along the way or give up hope altogether. But every person starts out with an innate longing to lead a life that matters. The "game is on" when we finally admit that we need to find something more. This admission comes with humbleness and with the understanding that we are still being shaped as persons. Our greatest joy comes when we unlock the secrets of our true identity, when we touch the hearts of other human beings, and when we build a lasting legacy of our days here on Earth. There is much rejoicing in heaven when a man regains his soul.

Who can adequately describe the soul? No one can, of course. But Parker Palmer provides an intriguing peek at this elusive entity. "The soul is like a wild animal—tough, resilient, savvy, self-sufficient and yet exceedingly shy. If we want to see a wild animal, the last thing we should do is go crashing through the woods, shouting for the creature to come out. But if we are willing to walk quietly into the woods and sit silently for an hour or two at the base of a tree, the creature we are waiting for may well emerge and out of the corner of an eye we will catch a glimpse of the precious wildness we seek."[2] Any sincere effort at soul-recovery must ultimately be made in the natural. It is here, in the dark forests and sunlit meadows, in the deeps of the canyons and the heights of the mountains—*in the wilds of our humanness*—that the soul conceals itself. If we are to discover

1. Merton, *The Wisdom of the Desert*, 11.
2. Palmer, *Let Your Life Speak*, 8.

our core of authenticity, then we must make the pilgrimage back into the wild—into the snakepit of the soul. It is a journey to be made not just once, but again and again, for as long as we live. It is the ultimate adventure, and if we are to be successful we will have to make diligent preparations and maintain an unerring sense of direction. There are certain habits that, if followed purposefully, can help us to find what we are looking for. Pulitzer Prize winning nature writer Gary Snyder calls these habits "the practice of the wild." He points to an emerging new wilderness culture, spawned from man's ageless kinship with the natural world and steeped in the habits of grace and freedom. Of the wild, Snyder writes:

> A culture of wilderness starts somewhere in this terrain. Civilization is part of nature—our egos play in the fields of the unconscious—history takes place in the Holocene—human culture is rooted in the primitive and the Paleolithic—our body is a vertebrae mammal being—*and our souls are out in the wilderness.*[3]

Somewhere back in time, as mankind catapulted himself into the future, he jettisoned something of inestimable value. Now, with the wilderness just a dim memory, this orphaned child of Nature finds himself without his soul. Like the Tin Man from *The Wizard of Oz* who had no heart, we too have an empty space inside—we are incomplete. Our souls are still out there somewhere, waiting expectantly for our return.

We know that the wilderness teaches the lesson of hope; that time and again, Nature presents us with fresh worlds of opportunity. It is never too late to begin the process of self-restoration—of becoming whole again. Encountering Nature with the compass of intentionality and a sense of purpose does not imply that her serendipitous appeal will somehow be diminished. On the contrary, these "habits of wholeness" will only serve to heighten the moment and deepen the significance of a wilderness encounter. They might be called the "best practices of the wild," but by any other name, *habits of wholeness* can help us to develop into fullness as persons. They can equip us to lay claim to our rightful place as the children of God. But before we consider these wilderness habits, it is imperative that we take a detour from the main trail of this book to consider the unsettling proposition that man is somehow alienated from himself—that he is separated from his soul. This will not be the easiest part of our journey, but at this juncture it would be wise to ascertain our present location

---

3. Snyder, *The Practice of the Wild*, 181–82 [emphasis added].

and determine a sound heading as we continue on together. As Abraham Lincoln once advised, "If we could first know *where* we are and *whither* we are tending, we could then better judge *what* to do and *how* to do it."[4]

THE MISSING ONE

A leading figure in the field of the psychology of man's missing soul was Jungian thinker, C. A. Meier (1905–95). In October 1983, Meier addressed the Third World Wilderness Conference at Inverness, Scotland. His topic, "Wilderness and the Search for the Soul in Modern Man," sought to elucidate the vaguely defined relationship between the outer wilderness of Nature and the inner wilderness of the human psyche. In his address, Meier posited that by his unrelenting assault on the natural world, the *microcosm* (Man) has been divorced from the *macrocosm* (Nature), and this separation has led to "widespread anxiety neurosis." If one were to develop a model from Meier's premise, it might look like Figures 6.1 and 6.2, which follow:

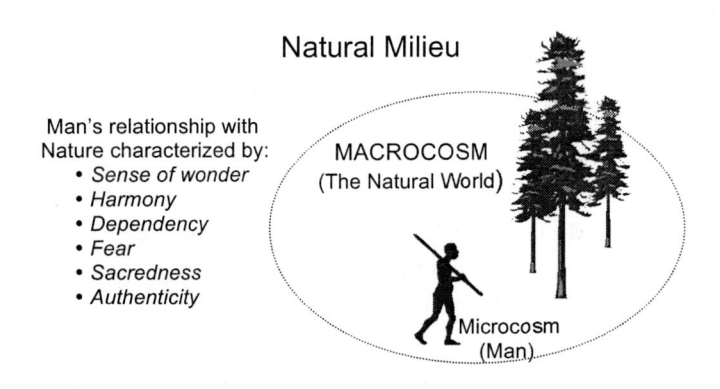

Natural Milieu

Man's relationship with Nature characterized by:
- *Sense of wonder*
- *Harmony*
- *Dependency*
- *Fear*
- *Sacredness*
- *Authenticity*

MACROCOSM (The Natural World)

Microcosm (Man)

In the *Natural Milieu*,[5] humankind enjoyed a harmonious relationship with his "Earth Mother." Man still possessed a child's imagination and the sense of wonder—that same innocence that Rachel Carson says we adults have lost and wishes that the good fairy would bestow on each of us. But when he "grew up," this prodigal son of the wilderness uprooted himself and

4. From Lincoln's famous "House Divided" speech, delivered on June 16, 1858 to the delegates of the Republican State Convention in Springfield, IL. See Basler, ed. *The Collected Works of Abraham Lincoln*, 2.461–69.

5. Jacques Ellul capably examines the terms "Natural Milieu" and "Technological Milieu" in *The Technological Society*.

moved to the city of progress and technology (the *Technological Milieu*). Emboldened by his will to control, man asserted his dominance over his Mother, eventually losing his primordial fears about her. These fears have been projected internally and, says Meier, this is the source of much of man's anxiety about himself and his final destiny. "The dangerous aspects of nature that kept our forebears watchful and humble have now almost disappeared outside; but they have turned inward (wilderness without, wilderness within) so that the whole of western society rapidly approaches the physical and mental cracking point from the inner dangers alone."[6]

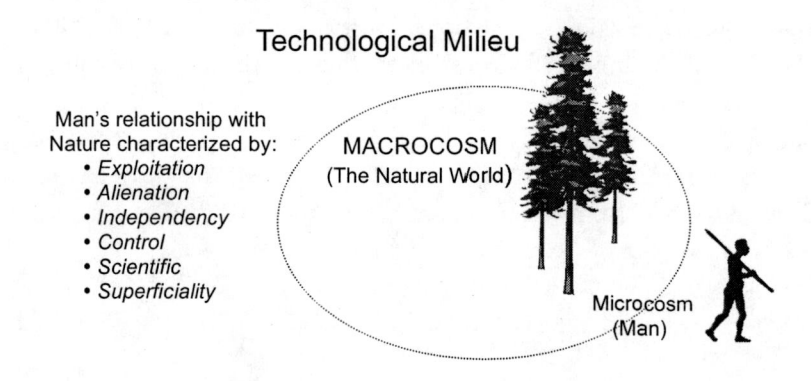

Technological Milieu

Man's relationship with Nature characterized by:
- *Exploitation*
- *Alienation*
- *Independency*
- *Control*
- *Scientific*
- *Superficiality*

MACROCOSM (The Natural World)

Microcosm (Man)

With our primitive fears completely internalized, Meier contends that should wild places disappear altogether, "it would inevitably resurrect powerfully from within, whereupon it would immediately be projected."[7] Meier's conclusions seem consistent with those of Richard Louv, who through his work in the field of child psychology has described the detrimental effects of Nature Deprivation Syndrome (see Chapter 1). While some readers may find these ideas to be somewhat clinical and overly pessimistic about our plight, they do aptly describe the nature of what Thomas Merton called "the great abyss that separates us from ourselves."

---

6. Meier, C. A., et al. *Testament to the Wilderness*, 6. See Meier's complete address (ch. 1) for a brilliant, if technical, analysis of the psychological ills caused by humankind's alienation from the natural world.

7. Ibid.

THE NATURE OF BROKENNESS

Merton's "great abyss" is a trackless wilderness, the metaphor for our separation from our beginnings and estrangement from the Source of all things. The abyss is the crack in our armor—our creaturely brokenness. While brokenness is not the most palatable topic of conversation for most of us, it is essential to an understanding of the human condition, and of the importance of Nature's restorative forces. The incredible power of the stories told in this book derives largely from the fact that the central players have been so utterly broken. My personal observations of human brokenness have been gleaned mainly from my professional career, assisting people who were between jobs, and also from my work inside several not-for-profit organizations. Most of the individuals whom I have counseled, while they have been particularly vulnerable, have also been open to a critical self-assessment and to the possibility of change. I feel certain that many of them have had a sense of being in *liminal space*. I am neither a trained psychologist, nor a therapist. In fact, I know precious little about the behavioral sciences. But two things I do know:

1. Every man and woman I have met has experienced some degree of brokenness in his or her life's journey. By brokenness, I am referring not as much to the hurts and sorrows that inevitably come our way, as to the crucial pieces that are missing—the plain fact of our incompleteness. This is demonstrated by our longing, whether we are fully conscious of it or not, to know who we are and to find a life worth living. Although most of my consulting experience has been with men, I have found that women are not immune to this same sense of incompleteness and absence of personal fulfillment.

2. Our hunger for self-understanding and our deep need to discover our gifts and callings are not being nourished by western materialistic culture. The disturbing facts and trends (which were identified in Chapter 2) testify to the abject failure of modernity to address man's spiritual center. This is a collective as well as an individual problem.

The brokenness I have seen manifests itself in one or both of the following: first, by the awareness that we have gaps in our lives; second, by a sense of guilt, regret, and remorse. Along with guilt and regret, many of the men I know also admit to feelings of anger. Oddly, when asked about it, these same men will tell you that they do not know why they are angry. I am firmly convinced that many—if not most—of us are oblivious to the undercurrents of guilt, regretfulness, and anger that are part of our present condition. Below are two real-life examples to support this contention.

Afflicting the Comfortable

A few years ago, a recovering alcoholic (not Roger) declared to the men of our Wednesday Group, "I have overcome my addiction. I have a beautiful wife and family. I am financially secure. I live in a nice home in a great community and I can honestly say that my life is perfect." Though he pretended to be convinced of what he said, we simply did not believe that everything in his life was "perfect." This man had become very "comfortable" with his lot in life, and we felt it our duty to "afflict" him with the serum of truth. So, the group sensitively challenged him to confront his sense of pride and make a sober reassessment of his situation. In the months following, there were several poignant discussions and "frontal assaults," which dislodged this man from his comfort zone. A year later, still sober and without any discernible changes in the environmental aspects of his life, he confessed, "I am a broken man! Without help from a higher power, I can't make it through even one day."

Comforting the Afflicted

Recently, I attended an important meeting of the faith community to which I belong. The church is in the midst of a very difficult transition, having had to ask its top leader to step down after sixteen years of service. The circumstances of his departure were very controversial, creating a treacherous "fault line" that has divided the membership by virtue of their loyalty or disloyalty to the deposed leader. At the meeting, a facilitator, who is an expert in the process of reconciliation, posed the following question for small groups to address: "How does God convince you of a deep feeling of guilt?" Before our table conversation could begin, the woman seated next to me could not control her disdain for the question. "Do any of you really feel guilt? Guilt is such a harsh word!" The response was immediate and unanimous, "Oh, yes! I feel guilt." Then, one by one, each of us compassionately gave personal testimony to the remorse and guilt we have known. When the topic of forgiveness was brought up, the woman rebutted that there were certain people whom she just could not forgive for the terrible things they had done to her and to her family.

Then, a hush fell over the table as I related the events surrounding a tragic automobile accident that occurred in the early morning hours of April 21, 1994, at the border of Idaho and Montana. On a mountainous section of State Highway 93 that was under construction, a pilot truck collided head-on with a passenger car carrying a 72-year old man and his fiancé. As a result of the violent impact, the man's lower leg had to be amputated. However, his bride-to-be was not so lucky. She was pronounced dead as she was being transported by paramedic rescue to the hospital. Following the accident, the operator of the truck maintained that the collision was precipitated by the elderly man, who was driving on the wrong side of the road. The man, who lay in critical condition in a local hospital, was unable to give his version of the accident until weeks later. When he was well enough to communicate, authorities visited him in the hospital recovery unit. Unable yet to speak, he was given a pencil and paper and asked several pertinent questions. Scribbling down just a few words at a time, he conveyed that he was driving at the posted speed limit and was on his side of the highway when the accident occurred. Unlike the young woman who was driving the truck, the injured man had an enviable driving record. The case eventually ended up in a Missoula, Montana courtroom. During the hearings, two independent investigators gave testimony, proving conclusively that the truck was going too fast for road conditions and veered into the oncoming lane of traffic. Under the weight of the overwhelming evidence, the woman finally broke down in tears and confessed that she had lied. She assumed full responsibility for precipitating the accident and said that she was terribly sorry for what had happened. After the proceedings, as the parties were leaving the courthouse, the man did something that was truly extraordinary. He approached the broken woman, placed his hand on her shoulder, and said: "You have been through a lot. I don't want you to carry this burden for the rest of your life. I forgive you!" The judge in the case subsequently awarded a substantial sum of money to the man, who gave every nickel of it away to support people whom he knew who were in need.

By the time I finished telling my story, everyone at the table was in a pensive mood, especially the unforgiving woman. As our meeting adjourned, she looked at me with tears in her eyes and said, "I will *never* forget that story." This episode demonstrates the difficulty and hidden nature of human brokenness. In the hubris of standing on the side of what we believe to be right, in being the "sole possessor of truth," we build barriers of isolation. This not only alienates us from others, it actually works to alienate us from our true character. We are no longer in sync with the Creation—as the Zen Buddhist would say, we are "out of Tao."

Towards the end of his life, when he could no longer saddle a horse or rope a steer, the man in the forgiveness story most enjoyed riding in his truck, far away from the little town of Salmon, Idaho, where he lived. I knew this man and when I visited him there, we had occasion to break bread, reminisce about old times, and have a few laughs together. Each day we embarked on new adventures, sometimes driving forty or fifty miles into the mountains to locations he had heard about and wanted to see for himself. As far as he was concerned, it mattered little where we ended up; it was the journey, not the destination that mattered. The man was content just to be present there, out in the wild. I noticed how anxiously he surveyed the countryside, looking for movement—a moose or a herd of antelope or a solitary coyote. At times, it seemed as if he had telescopic vision, gazing right past the scenic vistas that lay in plain view. I have since come to know that he was replaying his life—all of his life—and seeing beyond it to a better place. As you may have guessed already, the man was my father, and I am certain that in his time in the wilderness he found his soul; he got back into Tao. How else could he have known the deep wisdom of forgiveness?

HABITS OF WHOLENESS

Many of us would probably recoil at the suggestion that Nature's therapeutic effects go beyond a good day's catch of rainbow trout or a strenuous cardiovascular workout on a mountain bike. But the seeker who stops along the trail to admire the wild azaleas or smell the fragrances of the forest is uniquely positioned to derive certain tangible rewards from an experience of Nature. *Habits of wholeness*—paired paths to wisdom and enlightenment—that we should consider integrating into our lives are:

- Silence and Solitude
- Prayer and Contemplation
- Grace and Gratitude
- Forgiveness and Reconciliation
- Love and Freedom

Silence & Solitude

"With no birds singing, the mountains are yet more still." Most westerners, in our high decibel environment of machines and overpopulation, would be inclined to miss the essential message of this ancient Chinese aphorism. In our cities, the din of human activity is incessant, with little or no respite to hear the wind among the trees, or to listen for the sound of a calling bird. Even in our suburbs, Nature's soft utterances are drowned out so early in the day and resume so late in the evening that we are left with precious little time for quietness. Noise has become the bane of our lives. But this was not always the case.

There was a time in America when a camping trip was truly an escape from the hustle and bustle of city life. The family loaded up the station wagon with a tent, a propane stove, and a cooler, and then headed for the mountains. When they arrived at their destination they could expect to find other campers who respected their space and their right to a peaceful getaway. Unfortunately, outdoor ethics have changed since the heyday of camping in the 1950s. Nowadays, it is not uncommon for campers to hear nighttime revelers and loud music blaring into the wee hours of the morning. Scott Gediman, Yosemite National Park Ranger, told me that on one hike to Half Dome, he estimated that more than forty percent of the people he met along the trail were listening to music through their *iPods*. One of the consistent complaints received by officials at our National Parks is that cell phone reception is poor, or non-existent. The parks have begun to cave in, and it may not be long before digital invasiveness will have affected virtually every corner of Nature's wonderlands. It is probably safe to wager that the overwhelming majority of Americans are no longer acquainted with the meaning of silence.

Silence is the absence of all man-made sounds and artificial stimuli. Although silence can be achieved in other venues, it is found in its purest form in places that are farthest removed from the distractions of the city. Quiet places have a calming effect on us—disabling our defense mechanisms, tranquilizing our anxieties, and soothing our spirits. In my generation, perhaps the keynote voice for a return to the serenity of the outdoors was that of singer John Denver. Denver struck a powerful chord with his 1974 hit song, "Rocky Mountain High," which as it skyrocketed to the top of the charts, became the center for a firestorm of controversy. As part of the government's ill-fated "War on Drugs," the Federal Trade Commission

(FTC) threatened to ban all music that promoted drug use. The FTC began pressuring radio stations to drop "Rocky Mountain High" from their play lists and many stations complied. The song was reinstated only when Denver testified that the "high" referred, not to a drug induced state, but to the exhilaration of being in wild places. Though plainly written, the lyrics by John Lennon capture the essence of the wilderness in elegant fashion. As Denver sings, he paints a melodic portrait of a man in search of answers to the great questions he has about life's meaning. As he wanders deeper into the forest, his spirits start to soar and his soul fills with wonder. He begins to apprehend Nature in a completely different way. He now sees his life in a broader, richer context. For him, the sunset will never again be merely a sunset . . . he has seen "fire raining in the sky." The mountains are no longer simply masses of granite, but are magnificent cathedrals, where a man worships above the silver clouds. Denver's *seeker* comes to the knowledge that he is much richer for having experienced "the serenity of a clear blue mountain lake," and the sight of a golden eagle soaring high in the heavens. It all begins in solitude and with a listening heart.

John Denver left us in 1997, but his voice still sings the call of the mountains, to get high amid the trees and streams and meadows. Silence and solitude go hand-in-hand. When practiced together they are assured to put a person in a mode of full receptivity. We know from our lessons of the wild that being alone in Nature does not mean that one is truly alone, for the Presence is always there with us, the voices ever calling. Solitariness and quietude plug us in, not to the factitious world that we have become so accustomed to, but to the place of our deep belonging.

Prayer and Contemplation

John Muir affectionately called it "Nature's grandest temple," and he found the ideal place of worship in the Valley of the Yosemite. Muir was an inveterate preacher of Nature's creed, saying, "Everybody needs beauty as well as bread, places to play in and pray in where Nature may heal and cheer and give strength to the body and soul."[8] In his inimitable and humble way, he reminded us that we are part of something much bigger than ourselves. Although he seldom attended organized religious services, John Muir knew the power of prayer. Seeing evidence of the Creator all around him, a water ouzel or a bright garland of columbine was often enough to send him to his knees.

8. Muir, *The Yosemite*, 256.

Prayer can be supplicative, appealing to God to forgive us for the ways in which we have not lived up to his expectations. Prayers can be thankful, showing our gratitude for our blessings and good fortunes. Prayer is sometimes the last resort for people who find themselves in grave danger with nowhere else to turn. Such was the case for three men who some years ago found themselves lost in the Grand Canyon without water.

The trio was led by Steve Sample, an avid hiker who has logged nearly six hundred miles on Grand Canyon trails. Steve is no stranger to leadership challenges. Not only is he among the most respected university presidents in America, he is also the author of a best-selling book, *The Contrarian's Guide to Leadership*. But the situation that he, his nephew, and his son-on-law found themselves in, required more than just sound leadership. These men had departed from the rim of the canyon with plenty of daylight remaining for what was projected to be a straightforward eight-hour descent to a perennial water source in the canyon's interior. It was not long though, before they made a series of miscalculations that seemed to put their lives in jeopardy. Steve recounts what happened. "None of us had ever been backpacking before. We were taking what we thought were really rough, un-maintained trails. In retrospect they were paved highways compared to some of the trails that we later took. We foolishly didn't replenish our water when we had an opportunity to do so and we took a diversionary hike, which took up a lot of time. Now it was beginning to get dark, and we were unable to find our water source. We had lost the forward-going trail, and we had no headlamps, which was a mistake. All we had were two penlights, and we were on ledges . . . we were thinking we were going to die." As the men huddled together in the darkness to consider their options, Steve proposed that they pray for deliverance. In turn, each of the men gave thanks for his family and loved ones and asked the Lord to guide them to safety. It was then decided that the two younger men would take the empty canteens and the penlights, and backtrack to another water source, which the maps indicated was just a few miles away. Steve would remain behind to set up a temporary camp. At about 2:00 A.M., to his great relief, his companions returned with their canteens full. Incredibly, they had been able to find water in the dead of night without the use of their penlights, which had given out completely. The next morning, the three men easily found the right trail and discovered that they had spent the night just a few hundred yards from the water source where they had originally planned to camp. Although they had not been in the grave danger they thought they were, all three men came away convinced of the efficacy of prayer in helping them through their Grand Canyon ordeal.

Imagine for a moment that you have hiked for several hours up a lonely trail. You now find yourself resting on a granite overlook at the top of a high mountain peak. You can feel the wind in your face as you scan the horizon, which is so far in the distance that you can see the curvature of the earth, or so it seems. Wispy clouds waft across the azure sky, which has a vividness beyond anything that you have experienced before. The sun warms your shoulders, and you temporarily forget your fatigue and the sweat that drenches your shirt. As you recline against the rocks, peaceful thoughts begin to enter your mind, and you then remember why you came here. You recall all the truly important things in life—faith, family, and friends. There are memories of good times and bad times, of the many people who have been part of your journey—the ones who nurtured you, believed in you, shaped you, hurt you, loved you, left you. Inevitably, you come to the place of your brokenness, where you are confronted by your shortfalls, your failures, and your disappointments. You are faced by what it means to be human—point blank! You do not need to be an expert in prayer to do what comes next; an open heart is all that is required. You begin with these words: "Lord, I am broken and I need your help." This admission is your first step toward liberation—toward learning the seventh and most precious lesson of the wild. Below are the words of the Wilderness Prayer. It is all you will ever need to know to worship in Nature's grand temples.

The Wilderness Prayer

Lord, I am broken and I need your help.
Forgive me for what I have done,
and for the things that I have left undone.
Thank you for the eyes that witness your glory;
for the ears that hear still voices among the trees;
for the hands that hold the freshness of the morning dew.
I ask for the wisdom to know who I truly am, and
for the grace to discover my gifts and my callings.
Lord, help me to find the path that you have set before me.
I humbly implore you! Release me from my prison and
lead me into your loving embrace!
Help me! Love me! Free me!

It is time to remember the wisdom of the Psalmist, who millennia ago wrote: "I will lift up mine eyes unto the hills, from whence cometh my help."[9] In moments like this, a man is invited to move ever deeper into relationship with the Presence. This deeper state of being is called contemplation and it is the highest form of prayer I know of. Contemplation simply means, "the mind resting in God." Genuine contemplation is a true out-of-body experience, where a man transcends his mortal confines and is transported to a place of indescribable perfection. Contemplation is the portal of the soul. Muir says, "See how willingly Nature poses herself upon photographer's plates. No earthly chemicals are so sensitive as those of the human soul. All that is required is exposure and purity of material. The pure in heart shall see God!"[10]

Grace and Gratitude

Like silence and solitude, and prayer and contemplation, grace and gratitude are inseparable wilderness companions. Grace is simply the gift of something that we have done nothing to deserve; gratitude is the recognition of that grace. Without grace the world would be a much emptier place, and so it is with gratitude. The capacity to be thankful—even for the slightest of things—is one of life's great blessings.

Opportunities for thankfulness are often subtly presented and can happen at the most unexpected moments. Once, on a high country hike I found myself alone in the midst of a magnificent old forest of yellow pine and incense cedar. It had been a strenuous four-hour climb to an elevation of 7500 feet, where I was wearily making my way up the then gently rising trail that etched its way among the trees. I could hear the gentle whistling of the breeze and the calling of jaybirds as they flickered through the alternating shadows and rays of sunlight. I was daydreaming along, when suddenly I was besieged by a thunderous rolling sound, as if a horde of giants was crashing headlong towards me. My heart leapt into my throat and I tensed up with fear. It was then that I was given the answer to a conundrum posed thirty-five years earlier by a high school philosophy teacher: "Does a falling tree on a deserted island make a sound?" The teacher questioned whether or not a sound is really a sound if there is no receiver on the other end to hear it. I realize now that my teacher must have spent very little time in

9. Ps 121:1.
10. Sierra Club, "Mountain Thoughts, by John Muir," quote 19.

the wilderness, where the ever-Presence knows all ... sees all ... hears all. I hope that someday our paths will again converge, and I will be able to give the inquiring teacher the answer to his question: when a tree falls amid the peace of a faraway place, it makes a sound—no question about it! After the ancient pine had come to rest and the forest was still again, I laughed aloud at the gift of grace in the falling of a tree. It is fascinating to me that, although this tree had withstood the ravages of time for centuries, it toppled over only at the precise moment of my arrival. If I had come along a few minutes sooner, or a few minutes later, I would have missed it. As I resumed my walk, the tree was already beginning to surrender itself back to the earth in its decomposition, providing sustenance for other trees striving to reach the open space left by this fallen warrior. Just as Shel Silverstein's "Giving Tree" gave all that it had for its lifelong friend, so will this tree attain its fulfillment. All of life *is* beautiful!

The paths of grace and gratitude are more easily followed than other wilderness practices. Once you step into the natural world and find a quiet space, allow yourself as much time as is necessary for your city self to vaporize in the freshness of the clean air. Wait! Then, when the moment is ripe, ask yourself this simple question: *What am I grateful for?* Listen! If you are an earnest seeker and if your heart is open, I think you will discover that something magical is beginning to happen.

Forgiveness and Reconciliation

For many of us, forgiveness and reconciliation are difficult ways to walk. Forgiveness asks us to overrule our sense of pride and expose our flaws and errors for others to see. Forgiveness requires humility and understanding, virtues that seem to be in short supply in this day and age.

Reconciliation is the act of restoring a relationship. True reconciliation happens only when each party involved accepts ownership for their role in the division and agrees to meet the other on some common ground. The process of forgiveness and reconciliation always changes things. Even a relationship that has been restored will never be the same as it was before the rift was created. Genuine forgiveness and reconciliation implies tolerance for a wrongdoing. We tolerate the act because we value the person more than we value our pride. The forgiver is willing to give up the moral "high ground" in order to remain in relationship with the individual who needs forgiveness.

Two stories resonate with me when I think of the difficulties of forgiveness and reconciliation. The first occurred in the wake of a brutal attack on a truck driver named Reginald Denny, which became synonymous with the infamous Los Angeles Riots in the spring of 1992. The riots took place in the predominately black community of south central Los Angeles, as a backlash to the acquittal of three white L.A.P.D. officers who had been charged in the beating of Rodney King in 1991. As the riots escalated, four angry young black men yanked Denny from the cab of his stalled semi-trailer rig and then proceeded to beat the hell out of him. After bashing in his skull with a block of concrete and with several blows from a claw hammer, they mockingly left their victim to die in a pool of blood. The men, dubbed the "LA Four," were soon captured, tried, and convicted of various counts of assault and mayhem. Amazingly, Reginald Denny survived, but he suffered permanent neurological damage. At the conclusion of the trial, in a much ballyhooed courtroom scene, Denny approached the mother of one of his assailants and offered her words of forgiveness. He later appeared on a national television program to accept a personal apology from one of the young men who had beaten him to the brink of death. Fortunately, few of us we will ever have to forgive someone, as Denny did, for attempting to take our life. Reginald Denny's gesture of forgiveness was a Herculean effort at reconciling himself (and his assailants) to that which is greater than ourselves. The second case of forgiveness is no less remarkable.

During World War II, the home of Corrie ten Boom in Haarlem, Holland, became a "safe-house" for refugees who were fleeing from Nazi oppression. As a result of the ten Boom's activism in the Dutch underground movement, hundreds of Jews, Christians, and other Gestapo targets made their way to freedom. In February 1944, the ten Booms were betrayed, and several family members, including Corrie, were sent to Ravensbruck Camp near Berlin, Germany. When the war ended fifteen months later, Corrie returned home from the death camp and committed the rest of her life to a ministry of reconciliation. She testified to the liberating power of forgiveness, saying: "There is no pit so deep that God's love is not deeper still," and "God will give us the love to be able to forgive our enemies."[11] Ironically, despite having been tortured and humiliated on a daily basis in a Nazi concentration camp, she had yet to face her biggest test.

---

11. Corrie ten Boom House Foundation, "Home Information History," para. 8.

In the 1970s, when her compelling story was told in a best-selling book, *The Hiding Place*, Corrie ten Boom became an internationally recognized figure. She addressed audiences around the world, urging people everywhere to heed the teachings of Jesus Christ and forgive one another, no matter how grave the offense. One day after one of her talks, a man who had been seated in the crowd approached her, extended his hand, and asked for her forgiveness. It was then that she recognized him as one of the men who had tortured her at Ravensbruck. At first, repulsed by bitter memories of the pain and suffering he had caused her, she could not bring herself to touch him. But then she did something that marked her as authentic. She emotionally took his hand in hers and she forgave him. In that moment, one incredibly brave woman was finally set free from the prison walls that held her captive in her deep interior—in the wilderness of her soul. Corrie ten Boom is witness to what it means to be truly free.

Along with our individual need for forgiveness, there is a kind of corporate wrongdoing—a collective evil—that we all are implicated in, for which we need the Creator's mercy. In our relatively short time here on Earth we humans have caused irreparable damage. We have whittled away at Nature so relentlessly that wild places are now few and far between. We have marred the landscape beyond recognition and we have been directly responsible for the extinction of thousands, if not tens of thousands, of plant and animal species. There are few adults among us who do not bear at least some accountability for the present condition of our earthly home. We need to ask God's forgiveness for our carelessness and for our wastefulness. There has already been much said about man's detrimental impact on the natural world, so this book need not add more voice to that. But what this book does call for is a personal examination of our indebtedness to the Presence, who is the Source of our very being. This inaugural century of the new millennium should become our season of contrition. It is high time that every member of the human race work together to restore our relationship with our terrestrial Mother. Reconciliation begins with just one person—it starts with you! The next time you are on a mountain trail, or relaxing in a field of wildflowers, give thanks for what you see around you. Then, confess to your Creator that you are sorry for your part in the destruction of our planet. Commit yourself to the preservation of wilderness and to the conservation of all the living things that share our world. Reconciling ourselves to God on this score alone will have a powerfully liberating effect on us.

Habits of Love and Freedom

It may seem odd to think of love and freedom as habits. Perhaps they are not habits at all, but they should be! The succeeding chapter is based on the idea that love is the key ingredient in man's symbiotic bond with the natural world, and that the practice of love ultimately leads to personal freedom. The freedom we seek is of the rarest kind—the unfettering of our spirits. In a very real way we have become lost and we have forgotten the way home. Nature holds the key to the freedom trail.

Lessons of the Wild

- Self-awareness: *"I am truly alive and I have a wild heart!"*
- Humility: *"I am part of something much bigger."*
- Faith: *"I am not alone."*
- Tolerance: *"All of life is beautiful."*
- Hope: *"Life is abundant with new opportunities."*
- Honesty: *"I am going to die!"*

7

The Seventh Lesson

We shall not cease from exploration, and at the end of all our exploring will be to arrive where we started and know the place for the first time.

—T. S. Eliot

> In the middle of the land that is called by its inhabitants Koorma, and by strangers the Land of the Half-forgotten, I was toiling all day long through heavy sand and grass as hard as wire. Suddenly, toward evening, I came upon a place where a gate opened in the wall of mountains, and the plain ran in through the gate, making a little bay of level country among the hills.[1]

So begins the unremembered fable of *The Blue Flower*, which chronicles the adventures of a young man who dreams of one day embarking on a noble adventure. Then, in the aftermath of his father's untimely death, he has an epiphany that ultimately carries him to the ends of the earth. Standing at his father's gravesite, he fondly remembers his childhood and wonders what the future holds. As he visually measures out the family plot, he finds that a sapling elm tree has taken root in the soil above where he himself will someday be laid to rest. Recognizing that the tree symbolizes his fleeting youth, he resolves to waste no time in pursuing the

---

1. van Dyke, *The Blue Flower*, 11.

enchanting blue flower that haunts his imagination. By the time he arrives in the land of Koorma he has been on the road for several years.

As the gates part, a quaint little village comes into view in the valley below. Although it is bordered by desert, the place is an oasis teeming with life. Its well-tended vineyards and orchards are lush with fruit, and the flower gardens are "as bright as if the earth had been embroidered with threads of blue and scarlet and gold."[2] Tidy red-roofed cottages are scattered throughout the countryside, and the people appear to be prosperous and happy. The outstanding feature of the landscape is the deep emerald river that winds its way through the village and then branches out into every corner of the valley. In all his travels the wayfarer has seen nothing like the great river, which is clearly "the mother of them all."

As he wanders through the streets of town he meets a kindly old man who gives him lodging for the night. His host is a storyteller, who explains that despite appearances, times were not always so good in the land of Koorma. He reveals that previous generations of the village's inhabitants became corrupt and forgot about the Source of the river that gave them life. As a result of this ingratitude, the river dried up, and with it much of the community perished. As fear and uncertainty gripped the people, an unsavory element conspired to gain control of their hearts and minds. In those bleak days the village was known as Ablis, or "the forsaken place." When hope was all but extinguished, a stranger arrived in the village and told of an enchanting blue flower that grew in a secret location high in the heart of the mountains. The flower, he said, held extraordinary powers, and those who gazed upon it experienced miraculous things. He offered to lead them to the Source, where the flower could be found, and while many of the villagers were persuaded to follow him there, others became envious of the stranger's growing influence. During the difficult ascent through the steep alpine passes, the villagers fell behind but were guided by markers left along the trail. When they finally arrived at the Source, they were grieved to discover that the stranger had been murdered. But next to his dead body grew an exquisite blue flower. As they stood spellbound by its radiance, water began seeping out from among the rocks. At first, it was nothing more than a trickle, but as the days passed and more and more people made their way there, the river again filled its banks. The townspeople rejoiced at their good fortune and renamed their

---

2. Ibid., 12.

city, Saloma, which means peace. As the old storyteller continues to spin his tale of intrigue, he warns his guest of a "shadow that rests upon my thoughts," for there are evil forces still at work in the land of Koorma.

During his stay in Saloma, the young man befriends the storyteller's 13-year old granddaughter, a girl who is wise well beyond her years. He confesses to her that he is not at all like the villagers, who seem content to live out their days in the tranquility of the tiny hamlet. No, he is a "child of the unquiet heart," destined to wander until he possesses the bewitching flower that has by now become his obsession. He tells her that he once caught a brief glimpse of it in a faraway country, and that it was the most beautiful thing he has ever seen. At the time, the mountains rumbled, and he heard the sound of distant trumpets. But then the blue flower faded from view as suddenly as it had appeared. Wishing to help her new friend in his search, the girl proposes that they visit the Source where the flower can sometimes be seen. So, that afternoon, at the "hour of the visitation," they join a group of villagers on their daily pilgrimage into the mountains. Although this ritual is repeated again and again, each trip results in disappointment for the young man. Finally, the call of the wild becomes irresistible, so he says his goodbyes and resumes his journey. But as it happens, this is not the last time that he lays eyes on the place where a gate once opened for him in the mountain walls.

What are we to make of this peculiar old tale? Who are the players in the story, and what can we take away from their actions? What is the blue flower? And what, if anything, does it have to do with lessons of the wild?

FINDING THE FLOWER

The blue flower would seem to be nothing more than mere fantasy; that is, until we consider our own hopes and aspirations. In point of fact, the blue flower exists, but it takes a child's sense of wonder and imagination to actually see it. It grows in the high country and is visible only to those who truly believe. It appears to a boy in a vision, and is seen at the Source by people who have exercised great faith in getting there. The blue flower represents our dream. It is our hope that someday we will achieve something truly important; that we will make a difference; that we will find our place among the stars. To possess the blue flower it is to have peace. To be at peace is to be free.

I have met but a handful of men and women whom I suspect have experienced the pure essence of liberty. Such persons have a placidity about them that is inescapable. They make those around them wish that they could have a share in what it is that makes them so astonishingly ... peaceful. One such man is Thomas Keating, with whom I once sat for a few minutes, just before he addressed an audience in an old country church. As we conversed, I looked deeply into his face, and something quickly told me that I was in the presence of a man who was unlike anyone else I knew. Beyond his gentle features and his warm smile was a certain countenance that radiated a profound personal calm. He had this ... *aura of freedom*. I cannot recall the subject of our brief conversation, but I do remember that the man seated next to me made me feel worthy and hopeful. Father Keating had been invited there to speak about monastic life and the Christian practice of contemplative prayer. He spoke, and for more than an hour you could have heard the sound of a pin drop amid the throng of more than three hundred people who were crowded into the pews. Nobody moved; not even a whisper could be heard. There was only the sound of Thomas Keating's reassuring voice! He spoke with wit and wisdom, with humility, and with an uncommon perspective on prayer, faith, and the human heart.

Father Keating relates the story of the Sufi master who lost the key to his house and was looking for it in the grass outside. He was down on his hands and knees, running his fingers through the grass, when several of his disciples happened by and asked, "Master, what is wrong?" He replied, "I have lost the key to my house." So the students immediately joined in the search. After some time, as the sun grew hotter, one of his disciples asked, "Master, have you any idea where you might have lost the key?" The Master responded, "Of course, I lost it in the house." To which they inquired, "Then why are we looking for it out here?" He said, "Isn't it obvious? There is more light out here."[3] Thomas Keating posits that all of us have lost the key to our house and we don't live there anymore. We no longer experience the divine indwelling. We have forgotten the Source and we have taken the wrong trail.

Father Keating is a Trappist in the Cistercian order of monks, who adhere to the teachings of Saint Benedict.[4] For Trappists, as it is with other

---

3. Keating, *The Human Condition*, 8–9.

4. St. Benedict of Nursia (c.480–c.547) was born into Roman nobility. As a young man he rejected worldly values and fled the city to live as a hermit in a cave. He later established twelve monasteries, based on his principles for holy living. "St. Benedict's Rule"

monastic orders, the outdoors has long been the center for worship and communal life. In *The Human Condition*, Fr. Keating echoes a principal Benedictine maxim: "God speaks to us through Nature. The more we know about Nature, the more we know about the mind of God."[5] Monasticism, so deeply embedded in the natural world and so far removed from the clamor of the city, fosters silence and solitude, prayer and contemplation, grace and gratitude—the *habits of wholeness*. When wisdom is drawn out from the wilderness and into everyday experience, in the manner of a Father Keating, then all of humanity stands to benefit. Just imagine what life would be like if we had thousands of Father Keating's around the world showing us how to find the blue flower—showing us the way of liberation. Can there be any doubt that Thomas Keating is familiar with the ways of the wild?

A SACRED PLACE

The Source is a sacred place, and it is not by accident that it is hidden high in the mountains. A visit there is a pilgrimage into the wild, where once again we are confronted by truth:

- I am truly alive and I have a wild heart!
- I am part of something much bigger.
- I am not alone.
- All of life is beautiful.
- Life is abundant with new opportunities.
- I am going to die!

The villagers in our story do not have an easy time in making their way to the Source. But when they arrive there they are at the center—the place of peace. It is with joyous spirits that these believers make their daily walk into the high country, expressing their gratitude for the grace of the river of life. It is their faith that keeps the river flowing. When they gaze upon the blue flower the villagers experience raw beauty and they begin to see that they are participants in a much broader narrative. And while they are also confronted by death, they must know that they are standing

---

has become a principal influence in western Christian monasticism.

5. Ibid., 12.

at the nexus of life. Surely they understand the *paradox of hidden wholeness*—that death and life are two sides of the same coin.

The Source of the great river is found not only in the wild, but also within each one of us. What remains is for us to seek it out. Carl Jung once said, "Your vision will become clear only when you look into your heart. He who looks outside, dreams. He who looks inside, awakens."[6] If we choose to live by *habits of wholeness*, we will hear the still, small voice—the voice of the One who guides us on the trail homeward.

FARSIGHTEDNESS

It is ironic that he who most desires the blue flower cannot find it. The impetuous young vagabond thinks that the villagers lead a mundane, sedentary existence and have settled for far too little in life. But his fervor for adventure blinds him; he fails to see that the people of Saloma possess what he is after. The blue flower is right under his nose. How many of us are afflicted by the same far-sightedness? How many of us, like the young seeker, are looking for meaning in all the wrong places?

In the words beginning this chapter, T. S. Eliot provides a rich insight into the nature of the unquiet heart. He says, "We shall not cease from exploration, and the end of all our exploring will be to arrive where we started and know the place for the first time." Eliot was an exceptionally keen student of the human spirit, and underlying his words one will always find something much deeper. I think what Eliot is saying is that we lead our lives in a desperate search for significance and a sense of purpose, and that this search is driven by our basic hunger for the knowledge of self. At the end of all our worldly wanderings, if Eliot is right and if we are very lucky, we will come to know the person we are—our true self. To intimately know this person is also to know the Source of all things. To see this person's face is to see the face of God.

The story of the Blue Flower originated with eighteenth century romanticist, Friedrich von Hardenberg (1772–1801), who was an accomplished young poet and philosopher. He spent his childhood in the Harz Mountains of central Germany, where his family owned a large estate. The Harz has some of the highest peaks in Germany and in von Hardenberg's time it must have been a magnificent wilderness. American clergyman Henry van Dyke translated the Blue Flower into English in 1902. Like his predeces-

---

6. *Wikiquote*, "Carl Jung," unsourced.

sor, van Dyke was profoundly impacted by the beauty in Nature, believing that enough time spent in the woods would sooner or later lead a man to God. The themes of his books, *Little Rivers, Campfires and Guideposts*, and *Fisherman's Luck* attest to his lifelong passion for the outdoors.

THE HERO

In von Hardenberg's story, the central character is clearly the stranger who risks his life to lead the villagers to the Source. Without his knowledge of the blue flower and the mountain trails, the people of Saloma would surely have vanished into the vortex of forgotten souls. The stranger is our hero; it is he who blazes the trail and places ducks along the way. What sort of man was this charismatic leader? Why was he willing to risk his life for the villagers? Was he perhaps once like the young man—a child of the unquiet heart? Whoever he was, and whatever his intentions were, one thing seems certain—the stranger is a man of unusual character. He asks for nothing, but is willing to sacrifice everything to lift up the villagers in their time of tribulation. Then, Novalis provides us with a provocative twist. He tells us that the stranger is not really dead after all, and that he has been sighted by wayfarers in the wild. There can be no mistaking this man's identity—the stranger is no stranger to many readers of this book. He is the Presence, who is all around us, encouraging us along the way. We are never alone in Nature, for he is there with us . . . always. In leading us to the blue flower, our hero teaches us the seventh lesson of the wild. It is a lesson that makes all the sense in the world; indeed, a lesson that helps us to make sense out of our world. It explains why there is so much beauty in Nature and why Nature is our pathway to Paradise. The stranger could have had but one reason for wanting to help his friends. He did what he did out of love.

I am loved! I am loved! This is the great revelation from a lifetime of experiences in the bosom of Nature. This wilderness wisdom is perplexingly uncomplicated. It is right at our fingertips. It is the answer to all the riddles of existence. John Muir knew that he was loved. Thomas Merton knew it. Gerald May and all the rest, they knew it. My guess is that most of you know it, too. But Nature's most important teaching is merely an inconsequential tidbit of trivia unless men and women actually do something about it—unless they practice love, as manifest in the wilderness. Love is a calling that demands radical action.

PRACTICING RADICAL LOVE

I long thought that the man who gave the following account was a fool, but now I am not so sure. His name was Joe and he was responding to a question that came up in a seminar designed to help men discover greater significance in their lives. The question posed by the facilitator was, "How have you shown your love for your friends?" Joe was the last to respond. He began, "Once, I went on a mountain hike with some of my best friends. I was carrying a heavy pack . . ." As Joe went on, it became apparent that the group had misjudged the difficulty of the hike, and what began as an easy morning's jaunt through the woods became a full day's climbing adventure. When they finally reached the summit of their lofty objective, they were utterly exhausted and hungry and thirsty. As they broke out their meager provisions, his friends inquired about the contents of the large backpack Joe had lugged up the mountain. "I have something very special in here," he told them. Then, he ceremoniously opened his pack and produced the juiciest, most delicious looking watermelon that anyone ever laid eyes on. "What an idiot," I thought. Who would stuff his pack with a giant watermelon and then tote it all day long up a steep mountain in the blazing sun? Asked by the facilitator why he did it, Joe responded. "After what we had been through, it was the best gift that I could have given them." Joe loved his friends and he wanted them to know it, so he did something out of the ordinary. Guys like Joe practice love and they make all the difference. I want to live in a world full of Joe's!

If our existence happened purely by chance, then all bets are off—everything is a crapshoot; any trail will do! But if you believe, as I do, that there is a Source of life, then our world must have been created out of love. The Creator invites each one of us to practice the same love that accounts for a pinewood forest, a snowshoe rabbit, and a bipedal hominid blessed with the extraordinary capacity to give and receive love. What will it take for us to realize that we have lost the Sufi's key and that love is the way out of our wilderness?

WHAT HAVE WE REALLY LOST?

Back in the first chapter we examined the loss of the physical world, and throughout the book I have attempted to link the vanishing wilderness to our interior struggle for meaning. It is challenging to try to pin down the precise relationship between these complex domains, and perhaps we will never understand just how closely tied the two are. Although many thoughtful people are willing to concede that there has been a disconnection between the world of Nature and our inner selves, this separation is explained away as a necessary consequence of human development. It is well documented, however, that our progress has not come cheaply. One of the hidden costs in mankind's flight of fancy has been the erosion of love; not of romantic love, or of any sentimental attachment to the past, but rather of a deep, abiding love for the Earth, our fellow beings, and for the God of all creation. Signs of eroding love are all around us and they have produced barren spaces on the human landscape. The story of Ishi, perhaps as much as any other, portrays how love has been lost in mankind's long, arduous journey to the present day. It is a parable, not just of man's escape from his natural roots, but of the diminishment of his capacity for wonder and works of the heart.

Ishi was probably about fifty years of age when he stepped out of the Stone Age and entered into "the wilds of civilization." He was a full-blooded member of the Yahi, the southernmost tribe of Yana Indians, who had been ruthlessly hunted down by whites during the settling of the far west. The tribe was thought by anthropologists to be extinct, that was until August 29, 1911, when a fateful meeting took place in the early hours of dawn at a slaughterhouse near Oroville, California.

The butchers, stirred from their beds by the excited barking of the slaughterhouse dogs, could not have imagined the sight that awaited them as they peered out from the bunkhouse window. There, hunched tremulously against the corral fence, was the last surviving wild Indian on the North American continent. With his hair burned off down to his scalp and wearing only a tattered piece of canvas from an old wagon cover, "Ishi" as he came to be called, was a pathetic remnant of a time that had since passed. Near death from starvation, grief, and loneliness, he had "stumbled into the twentieth century," effectively closing the final chapter in the annals of man's familial association with the American wilderness.[7]

Authorities were summoned to the scene and they placed Ishi under arrest until they could decide what to do with him. Word soon reached T. T. Waterman and Alfred L. Kroeber, two distinguished anthropologists from the University of California, that a "wild man" was being held in

---

7. Ishi's story is masterfully told by Theodora Kroeber, wife of Alfred A. Kroeber (1876–1960), a leading ethnographer of the California Indian. See Kroeber, *Ishi, In Two Worlds*.

the Oroville jail. Before long, Ishi was released into Waterman's custody and taken to Berkeley, where a room had been prepared for him in the university's museum. During the next four years, Ishi was befriended by Waterman, Kroeber, and Dr. Saxton Pope, who became his physician. What transpired during those four years is probably unique in world history. It may mark the one and only time that men of the future traveled thousands of years into the past, escorted by its sole survivor.

Anxious to learn as much as they could about primitive life and customs, professors Kroeber and Waterman coaxed Ishi into taking them to the Mill Creek area of northern California, once the principal stronghold of the Yahi Indians. On a nostalgic journey back into his former life, Ishi showed them the important places of his youth where he learned the ways of his fathers. He led them on winding trails to secluded caves where his people hid from the whites. They visited secret Yahi camps, hunting grounds, and gravesites, where things were still much as Ishi's tribe had left them. With precision and artistry, Ishi crafted flint arrowheads and carved bows and arrows, then demonstrated his hunting skills with deadly accuracy. He showed his friends how to spear salmon with Stone Age implements, how the Indians preserved meat and fish, and the manner in which acorns could be processed to make them edible. The men swam in the stream during the heat of the day, then in the evening told tales of adventure and danced around the campfire to the tune of Dr. Pope's guitar.

Ishi had a jovial personality and in his own broken English would often ask, "Evelybody hoppy?" He had a playful spirit and he loved to tell stories, especially humorous ones. And while people laughed along with him, no one ever laughed at him. Once, Dr. Pope took him to see Wild Bill Hickock's Wild West Show, which Ishi enjoyed on several occasions. During the performance they were approached by a curious Sioux Indian, who was one of the participants in the show. He looked Ishi over very carefully before asking, "What tribe of Indian is this?" When told that Ishi was a Yana from California, the Sioux looked looked critically into his face and his fingers through Ishi's hair. "He is a very high grade of Indian," remarked the Sioux; high grade of Indian, indeed!

Although he was clearly a man for the wilderness, Ishi found contentment with his new life and often demonstrated his affection for his white brothers. He relished the opportunity to be with other human beings and seldom missed a chance to make an appearance when visitors came to the museum. Professor Waterman became so attached to him, that when the "Wild Man" died in 1916, he proclaimed, "He was the best friend I had in the world."[8] Ishi came to us through grace and he taught us much about ourselves. In the glimpse he gave us of prehistoric man, science learned—somewhat to its surprise—that modern humans are identical with their ancestors. Above all else, we need to love and be loved.

In the concluding pages of *The Blue Flower*, the young man returns to Saloma after ten years of fruitless wandering. But this time he is greeted, not by bright gardens and emerald rivers, but by pestilence and death. The people have again forgotten the Source and the riverbed has run dry. The villagers worship cisterns and wells and they must spend every waking hour in the search for water. Only Ruamie, the old storyteller's granddaughter, remembers the way to the headwaters of the river of life. And as she has done each day since she was a child, she visits the Source to pray for her people. While her prayers result in only a small trickle of water, she resolves to keep to her task until the river again flows out of the mountains and into the parched valley below.

Our story records that the blue flower is not seen again, and the "child of the unquiet heart" continues on his way. But as he departs, he says, "I think that long before my seeking and journeying brings me to the blue flower, it will bloom for Ruamie beside the still waters of the Source."[9] It is hope, yes, but it is primarily Ruamie's love for the people of Saloma that keeps her going. It was a stranger's love that first led her to the Source. It was love that Ishi showed for his new friends—the same love that inspires a man to carry a watermelon to the top of a mountain.

LOVE IS THE SECRET

One morning as he marched through the bitter winds and snow at a Dacau death camp, Viktor Frankl had a profound revelation:

> A thought transfixed me: for the first time in my life, I saw the truth as it is set into song by so many poets, proclaimed as the final wisdom by so many thinkers. The truth—that love is the ultimate and highest goal to which man can aspire. Then I grasped the meaning of the greatest secret that human poetry and human

---

8. Kroeber, *Ishi in Two Worlds*, 234.
9. van Dyke, *The Blue Flower*, 37.

thought and belief have to impart: *The salvation of man is through love and in love.* For the first time in my life I was able to understand the meaning of the words, 'The angels are lost in perpetual contemplation of an infinite glory.'[10]

So it is, standing at the foot of a giant Sequoia tree and gazing wonderingly at its mighty branches sketched boldly against the heavenly blue . . . we become as angels. We join the winged Legions as we sit silently in an alpine meadow, watching while a herd of elk pauses to chew on the whispering grass. We can be nothing less than the spirits from eternity when we find ourselves suspended in time, lost in contemplation, in the midst of the swirling currents of a spring creek. The wilderness is holy ground. It remains the last great place on Earth where a man can witness the Infinite Glory; it is that sacred space where a man experiences God's love, arrayed in never ending displays of size and shape and form and color. And it was made just for us . . . created out of love. Nature stands ready to surrender her deepest secrets. Go. Look. Listen. Learn.

As for me, the next time I am in the forest, I pray that I will again hear those familiar voices. And I promise to remember the wisdom of an old time preacher, aptly named Billy Bray, who swore that as he walked along the woodland paths his left foot whispered, "Glory!" and his right foot shouted, "Amen!"

Lessons of the Wild

- *Self-awareness:* "I am truly alive and I have a wild heart!"
- *Humility:* "I am part of something much bigger."
- *Faith:* "I am not alone."
- *Tolerance:* "All of life is beautiful."
- *Hope:* "Life is abundant with new opportunities."
- *Honesty:* "I am going to die!"
- *The Seventh Lesson:* "I am loved!"

---

10. Frankl, *Man's Search for Meaning*, 49.

A Wilderness Interpretation

Psalm 23

The Lord is my shepherd; I shall not want.
He maketh me to lie down in green pastures;
He leads me beside quiet waters.
He restoreth my soul:
He leadeth me in the paths of righteousness for his name's sake.
Yea, though I walk through the valley of the shadow of death,
I will fear no evil:
for thou art with me; thy rod and thy staff, they comfort me.
Thou preparest a table before me in the presence of my enemies.
Thou anointest my head with oil; my cup runneth over.
Surely goodness and mercy shall follow me all the days of my life:
and I will dwell in the house of the Lord forever.

Interpretation

The Lord is my Trailblazer; I shall never be in need.
He has shown me lush meadows; He leads me to still waters.
Here—in the wilderness, He restores my soul
and guides me along the right path.
Even though I must face danger and even death,
I will fear no evil, for I am not alone:
He is with me; He comforts me; He is my strength.
The Lord has prepared a feast for me in Nature's wonderlands.
He has taught me her lessons,
and I have been blessed by His grace!
Surely His love and mercy will sustain me all the days of my life,
and I will dwell in the land of boundless beauty for all time.

The Wilderness Prayer

Lord,

I am broken

and I need your help.

Forgive me for what I have done,

and for the things that I have left undone.

Thank you for the eyes that witness your glory;

for the ears that hear still voices among the trees;

for the hands that hold the freshness of the morning dew.

I ask for the wisdom to know who I truly am, and

for the grace to discover my gifts and my callings.

Lord, help me to find the path that you have set before me.

I humbly implore you! Release me from my prison, and lead me

into your loving embrace!

Help me

Love me!

Free me!

Bibliography

Abrams, Jonathan. "Kaman recalls childhood frustrations." *Los Angeles Times* (January 15, 2008) D4.
Ambrose, Stephen E. *Undaunted Courage*. New York: Simon & Schuster, 1996.
Bade, William Frederic. *The Life and Letters of John Muir*. 2 vols. New York: Houghton Mifflin Co., 1924.
Bailey, Eric. "Yosemite National Park: Sleeping in a bag or in a hotel bed?" *Los Angeles Times* (August 13, 2007) A1.
Basler, Roy P., ed. *The Collected Works of Abraham Lincoln*. 8 vols. New Brunswick, NJ: Rutgers University Press, 1953.
Becker, Ernest. *The Denial of Death*. New York: The Free Press, 1973.
Berry, Wendell. *The Unsettling of America*. Dresden, TN: Avon Books, 1984.
Blanchard, Jessica. "It's elementary: Male teachers rare." Seattle Post-Intelligencer (December 19, 2005) No pages. Online: http://seattlepi.nwsource.com/local/252612_maleteachers19.html.
Bly, Robert. *Iron John*. Reading, MA: Addison-Wesley, 1990.
Boy Scouts of America. *The Official Boy Scout Handbook*. 9th ed. Irving, TX: Boy Scouts of America, 1979.
brainyquote.com. "D. Elton Trueblood Quotes." No pages. Accessed December 16, 2008. Online: http://www.brainyquote.com/quotes/authors/d/d_elton_trueblood.html.
Britt, Robert Roy. "Why Johnny Can't Read: Schools Favor Girls." No pages. Accessed December 9, 2008. Online: http://www.livescience.com/strangenews/060718_illiterate_boys.html.
Brown, Dee. *Bury My Heart at Wounded Knee*. New York: Holt, Rinehart & Winston, 1970.
Bryant, William Cullen. *Among the Trees*. New York: G. P. Putnam's Sons, 1874.
Campbell, Joseph, with Bill Moyers. *The Power of Myth*. Edited by Betty Sue Flowers. New York: Doubleday, 1988.
Carson, Rachel. *The Sense of Wonder*. New York: Harper & Row, 1956.
———. *Silent Spring*. Boston: Houghton Mifflin Co., 1962.
Cart, Julie. "Camp outside? Um, no thanks!" *Los Angeles Times* (November 24, 2006) A1. Accessed August 11, 2007. Online: http://pqasb.pqarchiver.com/latimes/advancedsearch.html.
———. "As Americans Change and Age, Visits to National Parks Decline." *Seattle Times* (November 29, 2006) No pages. Accessed December 6, 2008. Online: http://seattletimes.nwsource.com/html/traveloutdoors/2003453655_webparks29.html.
Cass, Connie. "One of Every 75 U.S. Men in Prison." *Associated Press* (May 27, 2003) No pages. Accessed December 9, 2008. Online: http://www.commondreams.org/headlines04/0528-02.htm.

Bibliography

Chawla, Louise. *In the First Country of Places, Nature, Poetry, and Childhood Memory*. New York: State University Press, 1994.

Clyde, Norman. *Norman Clyde of the Sierra Nevada, Rambles through the Range of Light: Twenty-nine Essays on the Mountains*. San Francisco: The Scrimshaw Press, 1971.

Corrie ten Boom House Foundation. "Home Information History." No pages. Accessed December 30, 2008. Online: http://www.corrietenboom.com/history.htm.

Craighead, Frank C., Jr. *Track of the Grizzly*. San Francisco: Sierra Club Books, 1979.

Danforth, Samuel. "A Brief Recognition of New-England's Errand into the Wilderness: An Online Electronic Text Edition." Edited by Paul Royster. *University of Nebraska, Faculty Publications* (2006) 20 pages. Accessed December 12, 2008. Online: http://digitalcommons.unl.edu/libraryscience/35.

DePree, Max. *Leadership Is an Art*. New York: Doubleday, 1989.

Dickinson, Emily. *Poems by Emily Dickinson*. Edited by Martha Dickinson Bianchi and Alfred Leete Hampson. Boston: Little, Brown & Co., 1972.

Dillard, Annie. *Pilgrim at Tinker Creek*. New York: Harper's Magazine Press, 1974.

Eiseley, Loren. *The Immense Journey*. New York: Random House, 1957.

———. *The Firmament of Time*. New York: Atheneum, 1960.

Eldridge, John. *Wild at Heart: Discovering the Secret of a Man's Soul*. Nashville, TN: Thomas Nelson & Son, 2001.

Eliot, T. S. *The Collected Poems of T. S. Eliot 1909–1935*. New York: Harcourt, Brace & Co., 1930.

Ellis, Richard N. *General Pope and U.S. Indian Policy*. Albuquerque, NM: University of New Mexico Press, 1970.

Ellul, Jacques. *The Presence of the Kingdom*. Philadelphia, PA: The Westminster Press, 1951.

———. *The Technological Society*. New York: Alfred A. Knopf, 1964.

Emanuels, George. *John Muir Inventor*. Fresno, CA: Panorama Books West. 1985.

Farquhar, Francis P., ed. *Up and Down California: The Journal of William H. Brewer*. New Haven, CT: Yale University Press, 1930.

Fee, Chester Anders. *Chief Joseph*. New York: Wilson-Erickson, 1936.

Fish, Peter. "Old Faithful Versus the Xbox." *Sunset* (July 2007) 104–6.

Frankl, Viktor E. *Man's Search for Meaning*. 4th ed. Boston: Beacon Press, 1982.

Free, Ann Cottrell, ed. *Animals, Nature, and Albert Schweitzer*. Washington, D.C.: The Flying Fox Press, 1988.

Friess, Steve. "China grows beholden to skin-deep beauty: Prosperity begets boom in cosmetic surgery business." *San Francisco Chronicle* (November 23, 2003) No pages. Accessed December 10, 2008. Online: http://www.sfgate.com/cgi-bin/article.cgi?f=/c/a/2003/11/23/MNGG1393551.DTL.

Gameworld Network. "Decline in Visitors at Yosemite Blamed on Video Games." No pages. Accessed August 10, 2007. Online: http://www.gwn.com/news/story.php/id/11943/.

Gibran, Kahlil. *The Prophet*. New York: Alfred A. Knopf, 1966.

Greenleaf, Robert K. *Servant Leadership: A Journey into the Nature of Legitimate Power and Greatness*. New York: Paulist Press, 1977.

Hagberg, Janet O., *Real Power: Stages of Personal Power in Organizations*. Minneapolis, MN: Winston Press, 1984.

Herd, Andrew N. "A History of Flyfishing." No pages. Accessed December 16, 2008. Online: http://www.flyfishinghistory.com/aelian.htm.

Howard, O. O. *Nez Perce Joseph: His Ancestors, His Lands, His Confederates, His Enemies, His Murders, His War, His Pursuit and Capture.* Boston: Lee & Shepard, 1881.

Hutchins, Lisa. "Prairie Racer: The Pronghorn Antelope." No pages. Accessed January 10, 2008. Online: http://www.antelope.org/.

James, George Wharton. *Heroes of California.* Boston: Little, Brown & Co., 1910.

Josephy, Alvin M. *The Patriot Chiefs: A Chronicle of American Indian Leadership.* New York: The Viking Press, 1961.

Keating, Thomas. *Invitation to Love: The Way of Christian Contemplation.* New York: The Continuum Publishing Co., 1995.

Kilmer, Joyce. *Trees and Other Poems.* Georgia: Cherokee Publishing Co., 1994.

———. *Open Mind, Open Heart: The Contemplative Dimension of the Gospel.* New York: The Continuum Publishing Co., 1997.

———. *The Human Condition.* New York: The Paulist Press, 1999.

King, Clarence. *Mountaineering in the Sierra Nevada.* Boston: James R. Osgood & Co., 1872.

Kinney, James. "Park Hopes for Piece of Federal Funds." *The Saratogian* (March 23, 2007) No pages. Accessed August 15, 2007. Online: http://www.saratogian.com/articles/2007/03/23/today's%20stories/18117117.txt.

Kroeber, Theodora. *Ishi in Two Worlds: A Biography of the Last Wild Indian in North America.* Berkeley, CA: University of California Press, 1961.

Krutch, Joseph Wood. *The Great Chain of Life.* Cambridge, MA: The Riverside Press, 1956.

Leopold, Aldo. *Sand County Almanac and Sketches Here and There.* New York: Oxford University Press, 1989.

Loori, John Daido. *Teachings of the Insentient: Zen and the Environment.* New York: Dharma Communications Press, 1999.

Louv, Richard. *Last Child in the Woods: Saving Our Children from Nature-Deficit Disorder.* Chapel Hill, NC: Algonquin Books of Chapel Hill, 2005.

Lovejoy, Arthur O. *The Great Chain of Being: A Study of the History of an Idea.* Cambridge, MA: Harvard University Press, 1936.

Maclean, Norman. *A River Runs Through It, and Other Stories.* Chicago: The University of Chicago Press, 1976.

Manley, Richard. "Decline in Visitors Continues at Yosemite." *Billings Gazette* (March 29, 2007) No pages. Accessed August 10, 2007. Online: http://www.billingsgazette.net/articles/2007/03/29/features/outdoors/65-yosemite.txt.

Martin, Douglas, "Frank Craighead, 85, an Outdoorsman and a Protector of the Grizzly, Dies." *New York Times* (November 4, 2001) B6. Accessed December 10, 2008. Online: http://pqasb.pqarchiver.com/washingtonpost/search.html.

Martin, Vance, ed. *Wilderness.* Scotland: The Findhorn Press, 1982.

Marx, Leo. *The Machine in the Garden: Technology and the Pastoral Ideal in America.* New York: Oxford University Press, 1999.

May, Gerald. *The Wisdom of Wilderness.* San Francisco: HarperCollins, 2006.

McWhorter, Lucullus Virgil. *Yellow Wolf, His Own Story.* Caldwell, ID: The Caxton Printers, 1940.

Meier, C. A., et al. *A Testament to the Wilderness: Ten Essays on an Address by C. A. Meier.* Santa Monica, CA: Daimon Verlag and The Lapis Press, 1985.

Mendoza, Moises D. "Shrinking Forest Service fights increased abuse of public lands." *Pasadena Star News* (August 12, 2007) A18.

———. "National Forests Battle Trash, ATV's." *Washington Post* (August 24, 2007) No pages. Accessed September 15, 2008. Online: http://www.washingtonpost.com/wp-dyn/content/article/2007/08/24/AR2007082400232_pf.html.
Men's Health Network. "Boys' Developmental Differences." No pages. Accessed December 10, 2008. Online: http://www.menshealthnetwork.org/boys/factsheets/02-devdiff.php.
Merriam-Webster Dictionary. Online: http://www.merriam-webster.com/.
Merton, Thomas. *The Seven Storey Mountain*. New York: Harcourt, Brace & Co., 1948.
———. *Seeds of Contemplation*. Norfolk, CN: New Directions Books, 1949.
———. *The Wisdom of the Desert*. New York: New Directions Books, 1970.
———. *New Seeds of Contemplation*. Norfolk, CN: New Directions Books, 1972.
Miller, Perry. *Errand into the Wilderness*. Cambridge, MA: Belknap Press, 1975.
Mitroff, Ian I., and Warren Bennis. *The Unreality Industry: The Deliberate Manufacturing of Falsehood and What it is Doing to Our Lives*. New York: Birch Lane Press, 1989.
Muir, John. *The Mountains of California*. New York: The Century Co., 1894.
———. *My First Summer in the Sierra*. New York: Houghton Mifflin Co., 1911.
———. *The Yosemite*. New York: The Century Co., 1912.
Nash, Roderick. *Wilderness and the American Mind*. 3d. ed. New Haven, CT: Yale University Press, 1982.
National Basketball Association. "Surging Merchandise, Record Attendance Highlight NBA Success During Playoffs." No pages. Accessed December 10, 2008. Online: http://www.nba.com/news/merchandise_attendance_050601.html.
National Education Association. "Are Male Teachers on the Road to Extinction?" No pages. Accessed December 8, 2008. Online: http://www.nea.org/newsreleases/2004/nr040428.html.
———. "Attracting and Keeping Quality Teachers." No pages. Accessed January 1, 2009. Online: http://www.nea.org/teachershortage/index.html.
National Outdoor Leadership School. "About Us." No pages. Accessed December 5, 2008. Online: http://www.nols.edu/about/.
National Rifle Association. "A Brief History of the NRA." No pages. Accessed December 5, 2008. Online: http://www.nra.org/aboutus.aspx.
Neibuhr, Reinhold. *The Nature and Destiny of Man: A Christian Interpretation*. 2d. ed. New York: Charles Scribner's Sons, 1949.
Olson, Sigurd F. *The Singing Wilderness*. New York: Alfred A. Knopf, 1976.
Outward Bound. "Mission Statement." No pages. Accessed December 5, 2008. Online: http://www.outwardbound.org/index.cfm/do/ind.about_philosophy.
Palmer, Parker J. *The Promise of Paradox*. Notre Dame, IN: Ave Maria Press, 1980.
———. *Let Your Life Speak*. San Francisco: Jossey-Bass, 2000.
———. *A Hidden Wholeness: The Journey Toward an Undivided Life*. San Francisco: Jossey-Bass, 2004.
Pergams, Oliver R. W., and Patricia A. Zaradic. "Is love of Nature in the U.S. becoming love of electronic media?" *Journal of Environmental Management* 80, no. 4 (September 2006) 387–93. Accessed August 11, 2007. Online: http://www.videophilia.org/uploads/JEM.pdf.
Phelps, David. "Aging baby boomers leading surge in cosmetic surgery procedures." McClatchy Newspapers (October 22, 2007) No Pages. Accessed March, 6, 2008. Online: http://www.venturacountystar.com/news/2007/oct/22/bc-self-srs-cosmetic-surgeryms-8212-lifestyle-in/.

Rawlings, Marjorie Kinnan. *The Yearling.* New York: Charles Scribner's Sons, 1938.
Ritter, Malcolm. "Scientists Unravel Chimpanzee DNA Sequence." *Associated Press* (August 31, 2005) No pages. Accessed December 10, 2008. Online: http://www.livescience.com/animals/050831_ap_chimp_dna.html.
Rohr, Richard. *Adam's Return: The Five Promises of Male Initiation.* New York: The Crossroad Publishing Co., 2004.
Roszak, Theodore. *The Voice of the Earth: An Exploration of Ecopsychology.* New York: Simon & Schuster, 1993.
Russell, Carl Parcher. *One Hundred Years in Yosemite.* Palo Alto, CA: Stanford University Press, 1931.
Saint-Exupery, Antoine de. *The Little Prince.* New York: Harcourt, Brace & World, 1943.
Sargent, Shirley. *John Muir in Yosemite.* Yosemite, CA: Flying Spur Press, 1971.
Schorger, A. W. *The Passenger Pigeon: Its History and Extinction.* Madison, WI: The University of Wisconsin Press, 1955.
Schweitzer, Albert. *Albert Schweitzer: An Anthology of Selected Writings.* Edited by Thomas Kiernan. New York: The Philisophical Library, 1965.
Sierra Club. "Mountain Thoughts by John Muir." No pages. Accessed December 28, 2008. Online: http://www.sierraclub.org/john_muir_exhibit/writings/mountain_thoughts.html.
Silverstein, Shel. *The Giving Tree.* New York: HarperCollins, 2002.
Smith, Huston. *Beyond the Postmodern Mind.* New York: The Crossroad Publishing Co., 1982.
———. *The World's Religions.* Rev. ed. New York: HarperCollins, 1994.
Snyder, Gary. *The Practice of the Wild.* New York: North Point Press, 1990.
Sobel, Dava. *Galileo's Daughter: A Historical Memoir of Science, Faith, and Love.* New York: Walker & Co., 1999.
Spafford, Kevin. "Legacy by Design: Succession Planning for Agribusiness Owners." *No pages. Accessed December 6, 2008.* Online: https://tv.ku.edu/news/2006/04/24/family-owned-farms-decline/.
Stafford, William. *The Way It Is: New & Selected Poems.* St Paul, MN: Graywolf Press, 1998.
Stewart, George R., Jr. *Ordeal by Hunger.* New York: Henry Holt & Co., 1936.
Storr, Anthony. *The Essential Jung.* Princeton, NJ: Princeton University Press, 1983.
The Supreme Court Historical Society. "History of the Court: Timeline of the Justices, Oliver Wendell Holmes, Jr." No pages. Accessed January 3, 2009. Online: http://www.supremecourthistory.org/02_history/subs_timeline/images_associates/049.html.
Thoreau, Henry D. *Walden.* 20th ed. Boston: The Riverside Press, 1883.
Tournier, Paul. *The Meaning of Persons.* New York: Harper & Row, 1957.
———. *The Whole Person in a Broken World.* New York: Harper & Row, 1964.
Turner, Victor W. *The Ritual Process: Structure and Anti-Structure.* Ithaca, NY: Cornell University Press, 1969.
USA Today, "Girls Get Extra School Help, While Boys Get Ritalin." *USA Today* (August 28, 2003) No pages. Accessed January 4, 2008. Online: http://www.usatoday.com/news/opinion/editorials/2003-08-28-our-view_x.htm.
U.S. Department of Agriculture. *Agricultural Fact Book 2001-2002* (Washington, D.C. GPO, March 2003) 169 pages. Accessed December 6, 2008. Online: http://www.usda.gov/factbook/chapter3.htm.

U.S. Department of Health & Human Services, Center for Disease Control and Prevention, National Center for Health Statistics. "Births: Preliminary Data for 2003." *National Vital Statistics Reports* 53, no. 9 (Hyattsville, MD: November 2004) 18 pages. Accessed December 9, 2008. Online: http://www.cdc.gov/nchs/pressroom/04facts/birthrates.htm.

———. "Deaths: Preliminary Data for 2003." *National Vital Statistics Reports* 53, no. 15 (Hyattsville, MD: February 2005) 48 pages. Accessed January 9, 2008. Online: http://www.cdc.gov/nchs/fastats/deaths.htm.

———. "Deaths: Final Data for 2004." *National Vital Statistics Reports* 55, no. 19 (Hyattsville, MD: August 2007) 120 pages. Accessed: December 31, 2008. Online: http://www.cdc.gov/nchs/data/nvsr/ nvsr55/nvsr55_19.pdf.

———. "Deaths: Leading Causes for 2004." *National Vital Statistics Reports* 56, no. 5 (Hyattsville, MD: November 2007) 96 pages. Accessed January 5, 2009. Online: http://www.cdc.gov/nchs/data/nvsr/nvsr56/nvsr56_05.pdf.

———. "Deaths: Final Data for 2005." *National Vital Statistics Reports* 56, no. 10 (Hyattsville, MD: April 2008) 121 pages. Accessed January 5, 2009. Online: http://www.cdc.gov/nchs/data/nvsr/nvsr56/nvsr56_10.pdf.

U.S. Department of the Interior, Fish and Wildlife Service. No pages. Accessed January 4, 2009. Online: http://www.fws.gov/.

U.S. Department of Justice, Office of Justice Programs, "Census of State and Federal Correctional Facilities, 2000." *Bureau of Justice Statistics* NCJ 198272 (Washington, D.C.: August 2003) 27 pages. Accessed December 9, 2008. Online: http://www.ojp.usdoj.gov/bjs/pub/pdf/csfcf00.pdf.

U.S. Senate Committee on the Judiciary. "Children, Violence and the Media: A Report for Parents and Policy Makers." (Washington, D.C.: September 14, 1999) No pages. Accessed January 28, 2008. Online: http://judiciary.senate.gov/oldsite/mediavio.htm.

van Dyke, Henry. *The Blue Flower*. New York: Charles Scribner's Sons, 1902.

Wikipedia, Online: http://en.wikipedia.org/wiki/Main_Page. Note: *Wikipedia* is an online encyclopedic resource of the Wikipedia Foundation, Inc. Web pages can be edited by users of the website. Therefore, *Wikipedia* and its other related sites (*Wikiquote, Wikinews, etc.*) were never used as an exclusive source for quotes, references, or material used in the writing of *Lessons of the Wild*.

Wikiquote: Web-based resource of the Wikipedia Foundation, a self-described not-for-profit organization dedicated to providing a broad spectrum of free online information services. Online: http://en.wikipedia.org/wiki/Main_Page.

Wilson, Edward O. *Biophilia*. Cambridge, MA: Harvard University Press, 1984.

Worcester, Hugh M. *Hunting the Lawless*. Berkeley, CA: American Wildlife Associates, 1955.

World Wildlife Federation, "Free Flowing Rivers: Economic Luxury, or Ecological Necessity?" 44 pages. Accessed December 5, 2008. Online: http://assets.panda.org/downloads/freeflowingriversreport.pdf.